How to Work with People... and Enjoy It!

Jenny Bird and Sarah Gornall

Routledge
Taylor & Francis Group

LONDON AND NEW YORK

First published 2019
by Routledge
2 Park Square, Milton Park, Abingdon, Oxon OX14 4RN

and by Routledge
52 Vanderbilt Avenue, New York, NY 10017

Routledge is an imprint of the Taylor & Francis Group, an informa business

© 2019 Jenny Bird and Sarah Gornall

British Library Cataloguing-in-Publication Data
A catalogue record for this book is available from the British Library

Library of Congress Cataloging-in-Publication Data
Names: Bird, Jenny, author. | Gornall, Sarah, author.
Title: How to work with people... and enjoy it! / Jenny Bird and Sarah Gornall.
Description: 1 Edition. | New York: Routledge, 2019. | Includes bibliographical references and index.
Identifiers: LCCN 2018048879 (print) | LCCN 2019004646 (ebook) | ISBN 9780429465833 (Master eBook) | ISBN 9780429879807 (Mobipocket) | ISBN 9780429879821 (Adobe Reader) | ISBN 9781138610293 (hardback) | ISBN 9781138610316 (pbk.) | ISBN 9780429465833 (ebk)
Subjects: LCSH: Interpersonal relations. | Social interaction. | Psychology, Industrial.
Classification: LCC HM1106 (ebook) | LCC HM1106 .B527 2019 (print) | DDC 302–dc23
LC record available at https://lccn.loc.gov/2018048879

ISBN: 978-1-138-61029-3 (hbk)
ISBN: 978-1-138-61031-6 (pbk)
ISBN: 978-0-429-46583-3 (ebk)

Typeset in Bembo
by Deanta Global Publishing Services, Chennai, India

Printed and bound in Great Britain by
TJ International Ltd, Padstow, Cornwall

Contents

About the authors and illustrator

Jenny Bird is an acclaimed executive coach, working with senior leaders since 2000, and a coach supervisor. She is passionate about great relationships and communications in organisations of all sizes and believes that our real work is always with each other. She is known for her contributions to coaching standards and professionalism. A graduate of the University of Oxford, Jenny worked for many years in Adult and Community Education. She has been a speaker and facilitator at numerous master classes, webinars and conferences for coaches across the world. www.jbexecutivecoaching.com.

Sarah Gornall is an inspiring coach, supervisor, mentor and trainer, highly respected for her contributions to the coaching profession in the UK. She works with executives and coaches across the UK and internationally to develop resourcefulness, resilience and relationships. A graduate of the University of Cambridge, she has over 30 years' experience in Learning and Development. Previous books include *Coaching and Learning in Schools: A Practical Guide* (SAGE 2013). Sarah has been a Board member of several not-for-profit organisations, including the UK Chapter of the International Coach Federation (ICF) (President 2018–19). www.coachingclimate.co.uk.

Together their insights, models and methods support great coaching practice internationally. They are committed to the use of coaching principles to promote collaborative environments for human endeavour. Their previous book *The Art of Coaching: A Handbook of Tips and Tools* is hugely popular with business leaders and coaches worldwide.

Jess Balla is a freelance illustrator based in Bristol, UK. Her work focuses on bridging a gap between knowledge and understanding; often using a lens of humour to express how the human experience reflects our environment. She has worked for a wide range of clients including: Routledge, Surfers Against Sewage, Akram Kahn Company, Ottolenghi, Lush Cosmetics, musicians and independent businesses. Explore her portfolio at www.ballawaves.com.

Acknowledgements

Firstly, we want to thank each other: for being different and great to work with.

Then Dennis, for all the tea (Earl Grey please!), ice cream and cake. As well as patience and positivity.

We are also grateful to the following for permission to redraw and describe copyright material: Trudi Newton for permission to adapt the PAC model from *Tactics* (Napper & Newton Figure 4.3); the Taylor & Francis Group for permission to redraw (in some cases develop) material from our own *The Art of Coaching: A Handbook of Tips and Tools* (Bird and Gornall Routledge 2016), and Bruce Peltier's drawing of the Johari Window from *The Psychology of Executive Coaching* (Routledge 2001).

The illustrations in this book were created by Jess Balla. The majority were adapted from original sketches by Sarah Gornall. Josie Vallely, the illustrator of *The Art of Coaching*, generously gave permission for us to redraw several of her illustrations for this book too.

Thank you Jess: for staying so true to our intentions and for deftly creating illustrations from some ideas which we only gave you in words. We are grateful for your subtle skill in honouring our ideas and expressing them in your own engaging style.

Chapter 1

Introduction

Introduction

The carpet fitter punched the new carpet deftly into the corner and with great panache made a sweeping final cut.

"Well, I don't think they'll be able to replace me with a computer", he said. Then reflecting some more, he added, *"The rest of you will be working ten hours a week and I'll still be on my knees ten hours a day"*.

It was 1985. In our dream of a brave new world, computers would take over all administrative, informational, data and statistical jobs and most managerial, commercial and logistical ones. Many people would work only minimal hours accomplishing things which had previously taken long and arduous working weeks. We had earnest discussions about increased leisure, the impact on the entertainment infrastructure, health, spending and crime. *Everyone would have more time to talk to each other. Everyone would be happier.*

In the event, overall, the reverse has happened. We work longer hours, hunch over our computers and are constantly on call. The internet and information technology have made so many things possible. As e-communication is faster, we expect immediate responses. There is a mindset that because we can, we must. *Yet a huge percentage of people are unhappy at work.* Interpersonal tensions, circular discussions and poor communication between managers and the managed lead to disillusionment, demotivation and stress.

There is an iterative story about new technology. It has the potential to liberate us and, at the same time, it overwhelms us. Computers have worked out codes to allow us to decipher encrypted messages in times of war when our human brains would have taken too long. Algorithms run by computers have threatened the security of world financial systems. In the 1970s people talked about Artificial Intelligence and we debated how far computers could replace humans. Would computers be able to translate languages? Surely not. Surely only human beings could interpret idiom, register and the rich realm of language? Now, in the not so new millennium, there is a plethora of translation apps. Artificial intelligence used to be the stuff of science fiction: now we know that our cars can drive themselves and robots can not only relieve us of mundane, arduous tasks but also respond to us like sentient human beings.

And along the way, we have developed so many more ways to communicate with each other. So many more ways to trip up and miscommunicate. Face to face meetings, telephone and letters are no longer the only ways of communicating. Email, text, message, Twitter, WhatsApp, LinkedIn, Facebook, Pinterest, Instagram, Skype and video conferencing all offer opportunity, speed and global reach. They each have their own etiquettes and protocols, each impact on communication in different ways, each brings both opportunity and pressure. It can be easy to forget that the end recipient of all this communication is another human being.

Freed by technology?

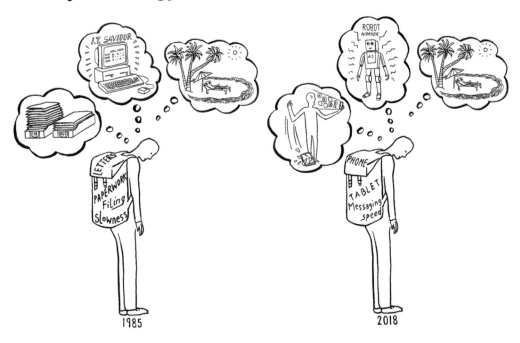

The more different ways there are to communicate with people, the greater the potential for miscommunication, distress and conflict.

Could life (and work) be different?

The answer is YES.

And a big part of what will make that YES come about is down to people.

People is not "them". It's us; you and me; how we interact with others; what we choose to do individually and collectively.

Long ago, someone told us that the two most important areas to focus on as a leader were the people and the money. Our experience as coaches brings us alongside people in all sectors of work, at different levels of responsibility. We support clients in times of tension, change, misunderstanding, reflection, resurgence and success. Time and time again, we meet people experiencing similar challenges who find that by looking inside themselves and relating differently to those around them, shift happens. So, the place where we are going to put our emphasis in this book is on making a difference in our personal and professional relationships, starting from the inside out.

A colleague coach tells the story of meeting a CEO who summoned his leadership team early one morning and took them to a top floor window which overlooked the company car park. *"Look out there"*, he said. *"See how they leave their cars. How they droop as they draw near and enter the building. I want to change that"*.

Organisations often say that people are the most important thing, but they actually put their emphasis somewhere else. This leader really wanted to make a difference.

In our work with people across a huge range of organisations, we've discovered the human face of the astonishing statistic that 85% of people just do not enjoy their work. So much of our time is spent at work that this seems a terrible waste of energy, motivation, idealism and skill. Because what happens when you don't enjoy your work? You start performing in a jobsworth way, don't seize opportunities, resist change, snipe at colleagues and take out your frustrations on those around you at home and in the community. What a vicious cycle!

No wonder there is such a high rate of depression. No wonder companies underachieve, in parallel with the individuals who work there.

We've had the privilege of working with many talented people, who have wanted to break out of this downward cycle, enjoy their work and their colleagues and have enriching relationships and great work-life balance. And they've often achieved it! So, this book shares some of the learning from our own experience and from working with our clients, in the hope that some of the ideas will help you enjoy your work more too!

Potential – Interference = Results

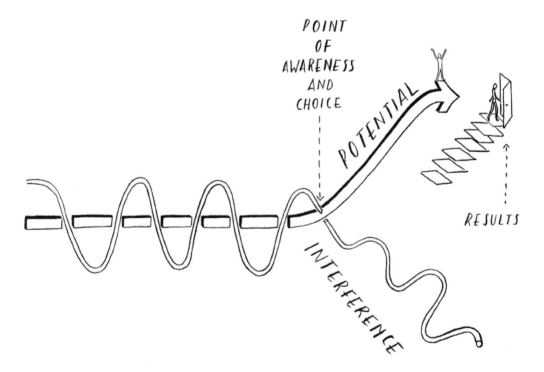

Results emerge when potential is maximised and interference is minimised.

Potential

The human brain is immensely powerful. Numerous processes are operating constantly; it is always active, even when we sleep. It is taking care of us, operating the whole human system and handling information from a huge range of data sources and stimuli. A number of subconscious processes are occurring at all times. The things we recognise as distinct thoughts are only a small part of this colossal activity. Individually we have huge potential.

Our collective world history is full of examples of success and progress; of learning about what motivates others, how to get the best out of teams, how to make the world a better place to live. As a species, we have enormous potential. Yet many of us live with the frustration of not achieving our best, either individually or collectively.

Interference

Things get in the way and interfere in all areas of life, personal and professional. Some people suspect that if they put more effort into relationships, these will be more successful. Yet they don't actually behave in a way that they know will make a difference. Others suspect that if they put more discretionary effort into work, they would enjoy it more. Yet statistics indicate that they don't. A variety of polls and research suggests that only a minority of people are actively engaged with their work. A worldwide Gallup poll conducted in 2011–12 in more than 140 countries showed that 63% of people in work were not engaged, 24% were actively disengaged (leaving only 13% who actually enjoyed their work). Five years on, in 2017, 85% of respondents were reported as not engaged. We observe that people who are not engaged are unlikely to offer discretionary effort to their employers.

What stops them?

And even more to the point, what stops us?

What might stop us includes:

- Myths and stories
- Assumptions
- Controlling behaviour
- Lack of self confidence

- Fear
- Lack of connection
- Poor or misplaced communication.

These interferences alter our behaviour in ways which we may not be aware of at the time.

What this book is about

This book is about maximising potential and minimising interferences to improve results and enjoyment both at work and in our interactions with other people more generally. It is about:

- Being yourself: growing, knowing and being comfortable in your own skin
- Recognising and accepting others as different: working with other people, their preferences and approaches to create synergy and results
- Developing collaborative and generative working patterns and productive relationships
- Replenishing and recharging before you run out of steam.

It will help you recognise what's going on and have more choice about how to react and what to do.

The sequence is:

- Know yourself
- Manage yourself
- Accept others
- Recognise your impact on each other
- Develop strategies for good collaborative working
- Identify watchpoints and things that can go wrong
- Experiment with techniques to improve interactions and overcome hindrances
- Stress test your model and create a personal approach.

It is a practical handbook with pointers for reflection, tools for experimentation, models for analysis of relational dynamics, tables and diagrams to stimulate personal and professional discovery and development.

Different assumptions – our story

Here's an example of how we notice our experience and draw learning from it and how easy it is to jump to assumptions. At the planning stage of the book, we, Jenny and Sarah, decided to work individually and note down our ideas about the structure of the book on a number of large neon post-its and then to pool, discuss and organise what we'd come up with. Off we went, in our own little bubbles of reflection. "Let's share now" we said, and then burst out laughing. Despite the fact that we've worked together for years and written another very successful book together, despite the fact that we know each other really well, we'd aligned our post-its the opposite way round. Sarah vertically and Jenny horizontally. Putting them together looked confused and disconnected. We realised yet again how easy it is to make assumptions, even when you know each other very well, so that you set out on even very simple tasks in a different way. The further you go without checking, the greater the chance of divergence and undermining the likelihood of success.

Assumptions exemplified

Simple words can so often be misconstrued. In a change situation at work, Mac the manager said to a line-report, when talking about her potentially filling a post with greater responsibility, *"You can't do that"* meaning, *"You can't just move into that job without an interview against the person spec"*. She heard *"**You're** not capable of doing that job, and I won't appoint you"*. It took weeks of stand off and union involvement to unearth the key.

We often make totally different interpretations of a situation and it doesn't even occur to us to check out these interpretations, because the way we understand things is so fundamental to us that it doesn't occur to us that there may be another view. It's not that we are deliberately insisting on our own idea, it's that we don't even recognise there could be a different one.

What informs the way we think?

The way we think is informed by a whole load of influences, starting from the time we were born. We absorb values from those around us at a time before we have a verbal memory, through observing those who nurture and care for us when we are tiny. These foundations form an unconscious hypothetical model of the way life works and how we have to behave to survive.

Layer after layer of experience corroborates our initial interpretation of the world. We match new experiences and challenges against our existing model and filter what we see and hear, tending to favour what fits with our model and to reject what does not fit. And along the way we form habits – habits of behaviour and habits of thinking – which we may judge to be unchangeable. *"That's just the way I am"* we may say, without taking seriously the possibility of change. What started as an approach which helped us to thrive, may have become a limiting belief which could stop us moving on.

Our experience of work and "the way we do things round here" also influences us. It lays down the foundations for new assumptions about the procedures, relationships, ethics and general way of being that is appropriate to the workplace. How we see others behave as leaders has a huge influence. We absorb ways of behaviour that we see modelled, even if our rational mind rejects them as ineffective in terms of received wisdom or in conflict with our values. When it is our turn to lead, we are likely to find that we already have ingrained behaviours which show up when we are under pressure and which we would prefer to change if we could.

We bring the whole person to work, in a holistic way. The mass of feelings, thoughts, habits, values, societal influences and views of the world that make each of us the person we are. We play our lives out in personal and family contexts as well as work contexts. We carry around a mass of internal voices telling us what to do. We are complex and wonderful creatures. And each of us is interacting with and impacting on other complex and wonderful creatures with a myriad possible permutations of outcome.

Some of the voices we hear offering ideas and judgements or exhorting us to behave in certain ways are internal stories. Some of them are voices from the past. Our mother's voice, our teacher's voice, our schoolfriends' voices. Most of the time, we don't notice all these voices; we think we act as one seamless person. And we often have a parallel lack of insight into the voices influencing other people too.

Six people in a conversation

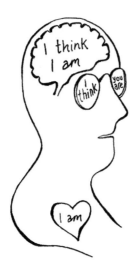 

Speaking at a debate with other contenders for the post of UN Secretary General in 2016, the successful candidate, António Guterres, was reported in the Guardian Weekly as saying *"When two people are together, they are not two but six. What each one is, what each one thinks he or she is, and what each one thinks the other is"*. He continued *"And what is true for people is also true of countries and organisations. One of the roles of*

the secretary general … is to bring these six into two. That the misunderstandings disappear and the false perceptions disappear. Perceptions are essential in politics".

As authors we bring

- Learning from our own experience
- Learning from our clients' experience
- Learning from our research

We have experience of life and leadership in all sorts of different contexts. We've made mistakes and had some great successes. Writing together sparks ideas and new thinking for us. We hope the outcome is useful for you.

We are both coaches. We both work across all three sectors – private, public and voluntary – in lots of different types of industry, at all sorts of levels of the hierarchy from the Board room to first line managers. We've coached people with national influence and new graduates in their first jobs, people with great ambition and people who have lost their way. We train and supervise other coaches, giving us yet more insights.

In writing this book, we reflect on our own experience and our learning from our clients' experiences. We learn from all our clients and think ourselves privileged to have such a variety of different perspectives. And just to be clear, when we quote a client, we have anonymised both the clients and their organisations unless we have their explicit permission.

Sometimes we read and research as well as talk! While other people's thinking and the findings of research are important to us, and we reference these in Chapter 8, we find the reading comes to life and makes sense when we reflect on it in conjunction with reflecting on our lived experience. It's a cycle of experience, reflection, reading, reflection, experimentation, discussion, distillation, articulation, experience, reflection …

This book is a practical work. We hope it will stimulate both reflection and experimentation.

Chapter 2

Finding the centre

Finding the centre

This chapter (indeed the book) starts with the self. The self is at the core of all we do and is the person over whom we have the greatest degree of control. Knowing, strengthening and choosing aspects of self to show or use in different contexts is the starting point. Working on self, with self, for self. Self-management and self-talk.

The impact of being ourselves and knowing ourselves

We all bring ourselves to every action and interaction, at some times more consciously than at other times. Knowing the self increases our choices:

- When we don't know self, we're not at choice, but acting on auto–pilot
- When at choice, we can manage responses and behaviours, and possibly impact on how others see us and react to us, so we have a better chance of getting more from ourselves and our working relationships.

Who/How Cone

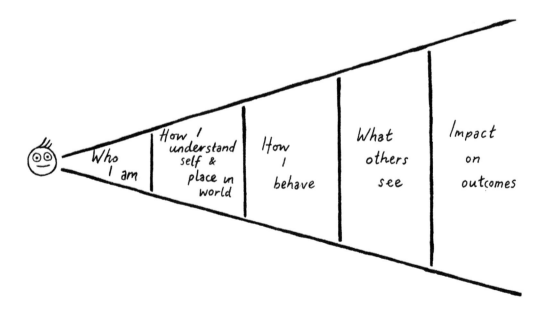

The *Who/How Cone* illustrates how our interaction with others and the outcomes we achieve start from our being, "*Who I am*". In this point of origin, we are just ourselves. All our understandings and behaviour expand outwards from this point of departure, as we present to and interact with others. Our self-awareness, "*How I understand myself*", opens out from this same starting point. Our behaviour has its roots here. The rest of our interaction with the world is amplified from these foundations with the cumulative result of our *outcomes*, what we achieve or create.

Here's an example. If I am the sort of person who sees herself as quick witted and as giving value by completing tasks really fast, there will be a knock-on effect in the way I speak to and interact with others. I may interpret some people's reflectiveness through the filter of my own understanding of myself, expecting them to behave in the way that I expect myself to behave, i.e., with speed.

My behaviour may seem to me to be businesslike, direct and appropriately paced. The more stressed I am by impending deadlines, the more this may be amplified. I may not give time to others to catch up with me. Indeed, I may not see why I should be expected to do so. All this is likely to lead to behaviour which is seen as bad tempered and rude by others, yet as natural and appropriate by me.

There is a risk that all my interactions will have that underlying disconnect and I will probably be dissatisfied with the result, perhaps even mystified. I might say "*I just explained to him and he took offence. I can't understand why*".

The more we know about ourselves and about how we show up to others, the more real we are, the more choices we have and the more confident we are to make the choices.

If we don't know ourselves, it's more difficult to know others, because all our perceptions of them are filtered through our own preferences and responses.

In starting with self-exploration, we open the way to integrity, trust and permission to be our true selves. We are each a unique mix of genes, history, feelings, thoughts and learnings. And when we understand what this mix is in ourselves, we are better equipped to work with others.

The ingredients of *who I am*

Be yourself: all the other parts are taken.

We've all observed different people doing "the same job" and each doing it in very different ways. Sometimes the results or outcomes are very similar, though the process, style, character and methods of work are apparently very dissimilar. Each person has applied their own equally valid approach, (although we may, because of our own preferences, think that our own approach is more valid than someone else's).

When we apply our real selves to our tasks, we can interpret our roles in a way which is authentic and congruent, and thus has integrity. And research has shown that what people want most from their boss is honesty and authenticity.

What happens when we genuinely bring ourselves to work?

Firstly, we can relax more because we are not playing a false role which is stressful to maintain. Of course, we still need to manage ourselves because we all have attributes which are not appropriate or useful in the workplace. It's not quite like the unmoderated truth: we don't want "myself, my whole self and nothing but myself", but we do want the essence of what makes each of us who we uniquely are, so that our colleagues can make a genuine connection with a real person.

While you may not want to show all your warts to the world, you probably want to bring the best part of yourselves to your work and connection with others: peers, colleagues, line-reports, customers, clients, suppliers, line-managers and all. The place to start is with knowing and affirming yourself. You can't be genuine with others if you have no sense of self-worth and no self-knowledge.

We each need:

- Self-esteem
- Self-confidence
- Self-knowledge
- Self-management
- Self-compassion

Hence, start with those inner parts of the cone:

- **Who** I am
- **How** I understand myself

As you build and accept what you know about yourself, you will become aware of the messages you give yourself about your attributes: these are messages springing from the level of your personal self-esteem and self-confidence.

There are three interconnecting elements here, self-esteem, self-confidence and self-knowledge. We define them like this:

Self-esteem = how we accept ourselves

Self-confidence = how we rate ourselves

Self-knowledge = how we understand ourselves

There is sometimes confusion about the distinction between self-esteem and self-confidence, so we hope it's helpful to differentiate between the two.

Self-esteem

People often talk about self-confidence and try to support and develop it in others … maybe with some difficulty. That may be because self-esteem underpins self-confidence.

Self-esteem is the knowledge that you are intrinsically worthwhile: loveable for yourself without doing anything. In most cases, it is the thing parents offer children the moment they are born, loving them just because they are: not for what they have achieved (as they haven't yet achieved anything!) nor for what they can do, nor for what they can give. Just loving and valuing them because they exist. It's the thing we would wish for everyone including ourselves.

What happens next? Many parents move from this state of acceptance of the child towards an expectation, or apparent expectation, that he or she will do something to earn praise, value, respect etc. So the child begins to take the message that they are only worthwhile when they walk without falling over, get high grades, achieve awards, are popular, run fast and so on.

We give people a gift when we help them to know they are acceptable just of and in themselves. This is a strong foundation from which to accept, value and respect others and a safe place from which to negotiate, compromise, create and collaborate. Without this foundation, other developments are harder. For instance, I'll find it hard to collaborate if I believe deep down that all my value or worth is vested in what I achieve alone or in competition.

Self-confidence

Self-confidence, on the other hand, is conditional on the belief that I can do things. People talk about confidence in two different ways. One is connected to confidence in a context or ability and the other is a more generalised self-confidence, which shows up in our approach to life and new tasks of whatever kind.

We can be confident in one area and at the same time lack confidence in another. For example, I may be a very confident driver and at the same time an unconfident navigator. This type of confidence about different tasks is often based on past experience or preference. It may also be influenced by the estimates of others, and we'll say more about that later.

A general level of self-confidence shows up as presence and willingness to try things out, a belief that I can do many things, even some I've not tried yet. The background to this is likely to be experience of doing well at a variety of tasks in different situations and possibly also being accepted as we do them and allowed to learn as we go. And general confidence may be vulnerable if someone is always measured against specific targets or against the achievements of others.

Knowing and growing ourselves

The section above was about how we might help others and how others might help us, but how we might help ourselves? How can we work on our own self-esteem and self-confidence?

There are ways to do so, which start from honest self-knowledge and acceptance. We can work on our own self-esteem, confidence and knowledge by honestly exploring what we know and believe about ourselves, our capabilities and characteristics, as well as our effect on others.

We will never know the entirety of who we are however, and this book is about growing self-knowledge rather than about therapeutic self-analysis. It is about knowing enough of our attitudes, approaches, preferences and personal quirks to understand how we can best be authentic, accept ourselves and others and foster productive working relationships and interactions. It's about making our working connections more effective and more interesting. Later we look at the range of ways in which we can get feedback on how we process or present, and on our preferences and patterns.

First let's look at what you honestly know and at heart believe about yourself.

Try this

Give yourself some time to acknowledge honestly what you know about yourself. Many people find difficulty in acknowledging their good, strong or effective qualities and how these work. Spend some time noting how you see yourself and what you know about yourself. At this point, just see yourself from the inside rather than how you may present to others. For example, *"I have high standards"* may also encompass *"I drive myself uncomfortably"*. Separate them out and acknowledge the connection.

Having high standards may eventually translate into *"I am demanding of others"*. For now, stick with your good intention about high standards and how it shows up in your own processing. While still staying with yourself (rather than effects on others) look at what you like about being you and what you might like to change or develop. You might be proud of and happy with your high standards and still find the demands you put on yourself burdensome.

Here's the example described above, set out in a table. As you consider what else you know about yourself, note what you see of your own attributes and consider how these might both add to your potential (➚) or increase interference (➘) for you.

Attribute		Application
High standards	➚	I produce good results
	➚	I enjoy the development
	➘	I drive myself uncomfortably
	➘	I find it hard to feel a task is complete

Return to this exercise from time to time to come up with a range of things you know about yourself. This is a work in progress. Over time we each gain realisations about ourselves and let them into full consciousness in varying degrees. Allow yourself to acknowledge what you are really pleased with and then also to accept the things which you know and don't especially like about yourself.

This type of self-knowledge is not self-congratulatory or boastful and neither is it uncomfortable and self-denigrating. It's just honest and interested. Imagine the best and most honest kind of appraisal with a boss who is utterly accepting, fundamentally thinks you are great and doing a good job and knows you can be even better and happier.

Jenny

I am very cheerful and positive. Once described as *"pathologically cheerful"* in an appraisal. Often described as inspiring. I value this in myself so that it is almost a condition of worth. It probably comes from childhood messages growing up with parents who had just been through a war: *"You don't know when you're well off"*, *"Look on the bright side"*, etc.

It's taken me a long time to recognise the potential shadow side.

- My constant offering of alternatives, options and solutions is often really annoying and unhelpful to others when they are not feeling resourceful.
- I am very hard on myself and experience feelings of self-disgust when I am not cheerful.

Awareness, self-care and choice

Growing self-knowledge will allow us both to accept the realities of others and to forgive ourselves, hence building self-esteem and acceptance. When we recognise the positive intention, we can be self-compassionate.

Our self-knowledge may be informed by a variety of processes. The most live and effective self-knowledge comes from being really willing to notice our own behaviours and thought patterns and consider how we may work with, adapt or develop these. This is a continuous process with layer after layer of awareness and noticing.

From live self-knowledge comes choice. Generally, if we don't know ourselves, we tend to behave in repeat patterns and (maybe) wonder *"Why does that keep happening to me?"* Indeed, we may see many things as externally instigated rather than the consequences of our own approaches, focus or actions. When we think that what happens to us all comes from external influences, we're in a powerless and frustrating place, where at worst we may see ourselves as picked on or repeatedly excluded and may even fall into patterns of behaviour which invite the sort of response we fear the most.

It's generally true that you get what you focus on, whatever this may be, at whatever level, the trivial or the more important. So, we need to make conscious choices about where to focus our own processes and perceptions.

At a very early age everything is of enormous interest to us. Toddlers discovering the world for the first time pay attention to small details without discrimination until these things have become part of their way of interpreting the world and interacting with it. They then select new things to pay attention to, assimilating previous information and detail and then moving on and putting their focus elsewhere. This process repeats throughout our lives. There is such a constant stream of input/stimuli around us that we are always selective in our perceptions, giving more attention here, less there.

Try this

Think about the shoe on your left foot. Now you have information about texture, pressure and temperature which you probably weren't noticing before. These were always there, and they weren't important until brought into focus. However, now it's likely that you will be more left-foot conscious for a while than you were previously and may lean differently on your left foot as you stand or walk for a while. There is nothing intrinsically different about your left foot – it's just that you have brought it into your consciousness more.

Try this

As another experiment, think of someone you are sometimes impatient with and find it difficult to listen to, and as result you often interrupt them.

Now tell yourself sternly and repeatedly that you must not interrupt this person.

Next time you have a meeting, notice what happens. Were you tempted to interrupt? Most people do interrupt, even when they tell themselves not to, because the concept of interrupting has to be created before we can contradict it.

Now, see what happens if you tell yourself instead to wait and to listen with curiosity.

In any situation, consider what it is that you actually want. In the example above, it is "*Listen with curiosity*". When we introduce the thing we don't want, we make it more likely we will get that rather than the thing we do want. This is because we have to create the image of what we don't want (however momentarily) before we create the image of not wanting it. And because the image of what we don't want comes first, that is what we tend to get.

Easier by far to create the positive intention first! Easier in terms of energy, more effective in terms of outcome.

Sally

As a 10-year-old, I was on a visit to my mother's valued friend and was asked to dry the dishes. Normally, I was sure-handed and dried china and glass with care. My mother kept on saying, "That's a really expensive cup. Don't drop it. You must make sure you don't drop it. It's irreplaceable!"

What happened? I dropped it on the hard floor, it shattered and my mother shouted at me.

Here's a few more instances:

- Tell a small child not to run. They will run! Telling them to walk is more likely to get the desired result.
- Tell yourself you can't jump across a stream because it's too wide. Then jump. You're very likely to land in the water!
- Tell yourself your boss looks cross this morning and will react badly. Notice how each one of his expressions reinforces that (self-imposed) belief.

As human beings, we are always selecting where to put our attention, either consciously or subconsciously, and as we do so, we interpret our place in the world. Our selections help us to connect ideas and make thinking patterns. These connections and patterns in turn help us to deal more quickly with complex new information and inform our response to different circumstances. The pitfall is that we tend to keep proving the same thing to ourselves. If we take the view that the workplace is unfair, we are likely to find the data to support that view. If we take the view that life is full of good things, we are likely to notice and celebrate them. The views that we hold become self-perpetuating. This is sometimes called confirmation bias.

Our biases are often influenced by familial and cultural contexts which start to shape our attention and attitudes when we are very young, maybe before we have a verbal memory. As a result, their hold on us is strong and forms the foundation for what we call our beliefs. Later they are influenced by our professional groups, the prevailing biases in the media and the community we live in. Surfacing these unconscious patterns of thought, filters, patterns and biases and examining whether they are objective or not gives us fresh choice about how to respond to the world.

The circumstances to which we respond are not the same as our attitude to them. It's useful if we have enough self-knowledge to separate these out to some extent.

We each bring to our world view the sum of our experiences so far: we might call this our baggage and filters.

Alex

Alex was walking past a shop as a small child and a goat unexpectedly jumped out of the door. As a child, Alex was scared. As an adult, Alex senses that this might happen again and may be anxious and alert for it to do so. Alex now has a filter (or perspective on the world) not held by many of us! Filters change the way we select which stimuli to notice and respond to. This filter changed the way Alex heard sounds and interpreted movements. And as the anxiety became dominant, it began to affect his shopping patterns and lots of other day to day activities.

What can this unusual example teach those of us who have experiences of failing tests and being shamed in front of others by autocratic teachers or line managers?

How might we filter our current experience as a result of our earlier experience? And what might we now bring to our presence in the workplace or our dealings with others?

We all have filters which are the result of positive experiences and we apply these to our interactions too. Where we have a history of being accepted and trusted, we expect people to be helpful, interpret their actions in this light and therefore approach them openly and engagingly. This sets up a positive spiral, as it is more likely that they will be positive in response. A smile tends to beget a smile. These virtuous cycles are part of the background of self-esteem.

Mike

Mike had received feedback that he was intimidating. He didn't intend to be and initially dismissed the suggestion. Then he chose to explore what he was doing that might make people feel intimidated. He asked for more feedback on what exactly he was doing that seemed intimidating and got answers like, *"You screw your eyes up and leave a long pause when I ask you a question"* and *"You sit sideways in meetings and drum your fingers on the desk"*.

Different people were interpreting Mike's behaviour through their own filters such as: long pauses lead to disapproval; not looking people in the eyes is designed to unnerve them; drumming fingers on the desk is a sign of impatience.

Mike had been scarcely conscious of his behaviour. He had developed these habits to give him space to think. Now he had access to a different way of interpreting it and could discuss with others if they could see his behaviour in a different way or if he could actually usefully change his habits.

Self-fulfilling prophecy

Our experience is good → we have a positive filter → we interpret actions in a positive way → we smile → we get a positive response.

Our experience is bad → we have a negative filter → we interpret actions in a negative way → we glower → we get a defensive or negative response.

As we work on noticing and developing our own processes and patterns, we expand our comfort zone, our openness to growth and our choice about how we might interact with others.

Try this

Think about some feedback that you have had. Consider which bits you are uncomfortable about and might like to reconsider and explore.

Ask the people who gave you the feedback to tell you specifically what it was you did or are doing that has led to this view. Ask, for instance, "When you say that I'm sometimes intimidating, what is it in particular that I do that causes you to think this? I'd like to understand".

Notice how you feel when you hear the replies. Are you defensive? What interpretation are you putting on the responses? What filters might you be applying? How might you think about this differently?

Consider the behaviour that is mirrored back to you. Is the picture consistent? Did you know you were doing this? What can you explain? What could you change?

Experiment with something different!

The experiment above looks at removing the interference caused by not recognising how our view of the world differs from others' (how I understand myself), what patterns we are replicating and how our behaviours may appear. We are gaining the opportunity to align our good intentions with what others actually see and understand about us.

Who/How Cone 2 – Observation and interpretation

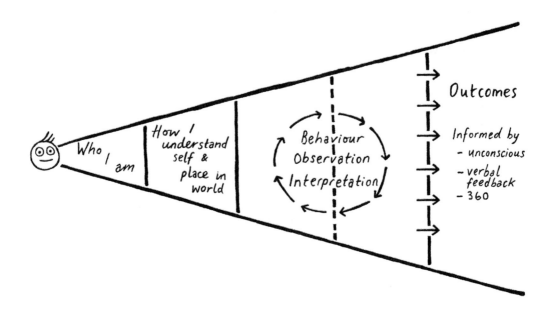

The next parts of the *Who/How Cone* describe **How** *I behave and what others see* (the 3rd segment).

How I behave has its roots in how I understand myself.

All our behaviour springs from our needs and self-care. This is very evident with small children. They don't cry without a reason. Their behaviour originates directly from their needs. Physical needs first, then social, emotional and spiritual needs at other stages in their development.

Later, in professional life, our behaviour will be founded on our needs and responses in that context. This will then be moderated by the feedback we get from others. We observe that feedback, interpret it and adjust our behaviour, then observe further feedback in an iterative cycle.

Ali

Ali is at a small conference. He knows that other people attending are more experienced in the field. He is keen to hear what they have to contribute so he keeps quiet.

His behaviour (keeping silent and waiting), which comes from a realistic understanding of his own knowledge level and real interest in gaining more information, may be interpreted by others as:

- Shyness
- Lack of interest
- Arrogance

And a whole range of other things, including the real one!

In the example above, if Ali has no feedback about how his behaviour has been perceived, he'll just carry on with how he is responding. As he interacts with others, and if he is able to interpret signals and hear feedback, he will understand that his intention was not necessarily visible to others and so he will have choices of response in future. This is the interplay between sections 3 and 4 of the *Who/How Cone*.

Who/How Cone 3 – Feedback and growth

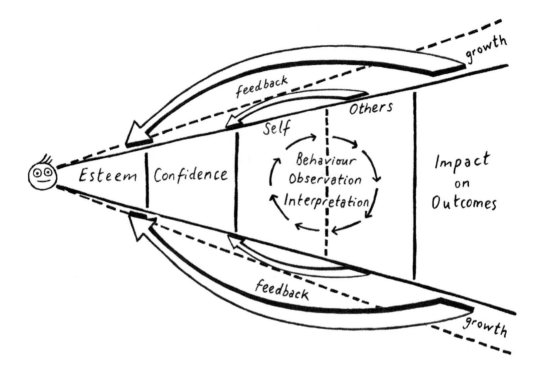

People observe, interpret and respond to each other in a developing cycle so that the feedback data they are able to receive allows them to adjust their input to gain different interactions and results.

There are numerous examples of the interpretation of one person's actions or words being unimaginably (to them) different from their intention. Star crossed lovers often experience this! When Sam says, "Keep in touch", Robin hears, "I'm being vague because I'm not really interested and want to be polite". Sam really means, "I really want to see you again but am anxious about being too pushy".

The realisation that others see the world differently from us and interpret our behaviour through filters alien to our own is often a revelation.

Fran

Fran, a function leader in a large company, was on a leadership programme for key people in the organisation. She and her colleagues were creating a presentation together. They had hardly known each other before the course. As they worked together she was amazed to find that the others did not share her assumption on how they would present their ideas and even more amazed when they greeted her thoughts as original and impressive and adopted her process with enthusiasm.

She said, *"I thought it was the obvious way to do it. I was thrilled to get such great feedback for something which seemed easy to me. And it was a revelation to know that people think so differently. It makes me more confident of the value of my ideas and keener to hear how others see things"*.

As we work on our self-knowledge, through the feedback loop between our behaviour and how it is experienced by others (sections 3 and 4 of the *Who/How Cone 3*), we develop more choices of behaviour which in turn create more possibilities for outcomes. We are beginning to reduce interference caused by knee-jerk reactions and ingrained patterns.

To recognise and use this process we need to notice our own interpretations and how these affect our behaviour and also to be willing to check how others are interpreting our input. We need to be willing to withhold our own immediate responses and explore what may be going on in the loop which goes:

1. I see.
2. I interpret.
3. I respond, acting on my interpretation.

Seb

Seb was invited to a selection centre for a panel role he was very interested in. The selection centre involved a series of interactive activities in small groups, observed by the selectors. Seb hugely enjoys this type of group activity and working with others so joined in enthusiastically.

He was not selected, and the feedback was that he had appeared nervous. Since Seb had not been nervous he asked the useful question, "What behaviour of mine led you to think I was nervous?" and was told that he had laughed frequently.

Though it made no difference on that occasion because the decision was already made, this gave Seb a choice for the future. He laughed because he was enjoying the process and connecting with others in the group. Now he knows that laughing in a selection process may well be interpreted as discomfort. He can choose a different approach.

If we don't know something about ourselves, the way we process, how our world view and preferred ways of working may differ from others, what hijacks us and what nourishes us, we won't be able to flex to work with others or even to understand what is happening when what seems like a simple communication goes awry.

Hilary: I'd like him to bring to bring me flowers occasionally … not every week, just sometimes. It's not much to ask.

Logan: Have you asked?

Hilary: No. He should know.

Logan: How should he know? Would **he** like flowers?

Hilary: No of course not!

Logan: Then how would he know?

In our work relationship as in our personal ones, we don't all want the same things or work in the same ways. So, if we start with some understanding of ourselves, our own uniqueness, then we gain a perspective which will serve us and others well.

Projecting onto others the belief that they are approaching things and understanding the world in just the way we do, will cause us (and them perhaps) considerable confusion. Here is an example of a real conversation in an English village in 2014:

Host: Would you like some quiche?

Guest: Please could you tell me what's in it?

Host: I'll check, why?

Guest: I don't eat meat.

Host checks: It's bacon and cheese.

Guest: Thanks. I'll just have salad then please.

Host: But it's only bacon.

Guest: Thanks, but I don't eat meat.

Host: Well what **do** you eat then?

Guest: Anything **but** meat.

Both host and guest were pretty confused by the end of this and unlikely to eat together again! The filters at work here included; what counts as meat: reasons for choosing what to eat: you can't refuse food in my home. Something which you think of as just the natural order of how things work, may be an optional extra to someone else.

Other people's perception of me

Our understanding of ourselves and of what we are worth, is inevitably influenced by the things people say to us and by how they behave towards us. We watch and listen from an early age, making interpretations and hypotheses on the basis of what we hear and observe.

If our significant adults greeted us with smiles when we were toddlers, we are more likely to feel that we are welcome later in life. If our mistakes were treated as learning opportunities, we are more likely to persevere when things go wrong. Being told we are a nuisance or clumsy as a child may negatively influence the picture we hold of ourselves and our place in the world as adults. Being scolded for mistakes may lead to desperate attempts to get things right first time and self-disgust when we don't.

What happens at home is often reinforced by what happens in school and in the wider community. There is often a tendency to discount rather than to praise, to blame rather than to accept. The stories we tell ourselves are built on experience and they often follow a pattern of reinforcing negative views rather than positive ones. Sometimes these perceptions loom so large that they prevent us developing a true sense of who we are.

Obscured view of me

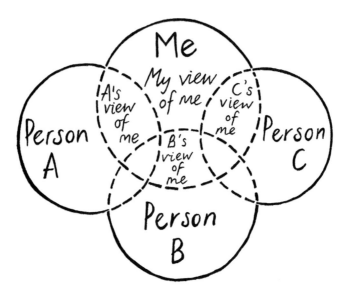

The diagram opposite shows how the views of others impinge dangerously on my perception of self.

When we are uncertain of our own truth and validity, we seek other people's approval and praise in order to reinforce our sense of self-worth. We seek external validation to a disproportionate extent and may be inappropriately swayed by it.

Marvellously, when we are secure in our place in the world, we are able to validate ourselves, to give ourselves strong messages about our worth and right to exist. We get a more balanced picture of who we are, which builds on our own understanding and is less susceptible to over-reliance on other people's views. Finding the ability to do this can help us relax, drop anxiety, be natural and contribute fully. It's a virtuous spiral.

Balancing the impact of others' views allows fuller expression of our own understanding of ourselves.

Clear view of me

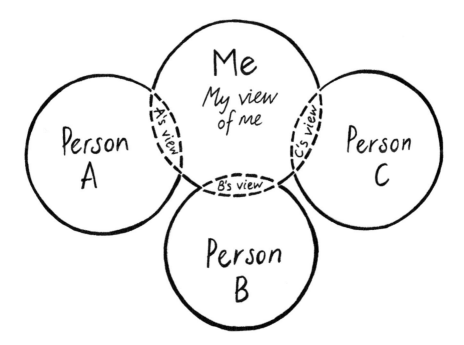

Stories we tell ourselves

Human beings are good at stories!

- Stories we tell ourselves about ourselves
- Stories we have about how the world works
- Stories we have about others and how they see us

It's useful to build both self-knowledge and self-compassion by noticing that many of these stories are just … stories. Not the truth, just a possible perspective, and often not a useful one.

Notice some of the unhelpful stories you might be telling yourself, such as:

- I've never been good with money.
- People like me don't do that.
- I haven't got time.
- I hate doing presentations.
- I'm not a cook.
- I'm slow at this.
- I'm always bottom of the heap.
- I'm useless with I.T.
- I can't explain clearly.

Many of these become self-fulfilling prophesies. We tend to act up to our own and other people's views of who we are and what we can do. We may repeat them and reinforce them. This is how it goes: we think we can't do something so maybe we don't try, or we tell someone else we can't, and they don't ask us or don't trust us to do it, because they, like most people, take us at our own evaluation. We think we're not good at something, so we approach it tentatively and watch out for our own mistakes and expect them.

So, when mistakes do happen, rather than thinking, *"Ok, so it doesn't work that way, what else can I try?"*, we think, *"Ah, I knew I was no good at this!"*

And in that instance, we're not! An example of "you get what you focus on".

Some of our stories come from the past, from our parents' expectations of us, things we heard as we grew and maybe things we adopted to keep ourselves safe. It's worth checking out these stories and letting them go if they aren't helpful.

Max

Max had a story that he wasn't good at maths. This came from a couple of lowish grades at school and a teacher who told him that he was amazed he passed at all. He offered this idea to colleagues, one of whom actually trying to support him, made a gentle joke of it and often came to check he'd got things covered.

When he was actually able to sit back and look at the evidence, he realised that, though he might not know a formula for a spreadsheet or how to reverse calculate a percentage, when he looked at data for his department, he could tell at a glance that for instance one sales figure was lower than it should be and another higher. This came from experience and what felt to him like instinct.

As he began to trust these "hunches" his confidence grew and he began to present himself more confidently to colleagues … who began to take him at his own (new) evaluation. Their acceptance further reinforced his new story about his capability.

What Max did was to reframe his story "I'm no good at maths" to "I can easily understand the data I need". We can all use this type of reframing process sometimes.

Try this

Follow the 5 stages in Max's reframing process.

1.   Identify the old belief.
2.   Check how true and useful it is to you.
3.   Decide what would be more useful now.
4.   Play with the wording until it sounds right.
5.   Remind yourself regularly until the new belief replaces the old one.

	Max's reframe	*Your reframe*
1	I'm no good at maths.	
2	Might be true about theory, but it's not true or useful in practical terms at work.	
3	I know what's right and wrong as soon as I look at the sales figures.	
4	I can easily understand the data I need.	
5	I can easily understand the data I need.	

Repetition helps new neural pathways to establish themselves. These are pathways from one part of the brain to another, facilitating the development of different patterns of thought. As we repeat them, they can become our default way of thinking. It's ideal if the default patterns are ones which support rather than undermine us. So watch out for what you choose to repeat!

We can create pathways which validate us. Establishing these as our default way of thinking may require conscious effort at first. It can be very helpful to have someone, maybe a friend, colleague or coach, to support us in the change we want to achieve.

Another useful strategy is to accept that you were doing the best you could at the time, which is useful in reframing our acceptance of ourselves and in dealing with others.

Try saying to yourself in times of regret and recrimination: *I was doing the best I could do at that time and/or in those circumstances – and what can I do now?*

This approach helps us to be resourceful, taking us away from focusing on our mistakes and regrets from the past into possibilities for the future. It expresses the belief that we can all develop and grow and that we are not trapped for ever in how we are now.

If we keep focusing on our mistakes, we are visualising them and are more likely to repeat them. This is also creating a neural pathway. The only useful reason for reminding ourselves of things which did not go well is to learn from them so that we have more choice in future and can try out new strategies. When you lose, don't lose the lesson. So the resourceful response to something which isn't how we'd like it to be is *"It didn't work that way, what else can I try?"*

Cycles of thought

Our interpretations of external events create thought sequences which reverberate throughout our personal and professional lives. These cycles of thought can be positive, negative or neutral.

When we make a mistake, we might react in a way which amplifies self-blame, negative patterns of thought and feeling. The small mistake leads to bigger ones.

Alternatively, we might react in a more positive way, seeing the cup as half full rather than half empty. The mistake is a stepping stone to success.

Negative cycle

The negative cycle shows how we might react to a mistake, blaming ourselves and withdrawing from the situation. This behaviour may further undermine our self-confidence, so we expect to fail and catastrophise in advance.

- *I hit a terrible shot.*
- *My backhand's useless.*
- *I'm a lousy tennis player.*
- *I'm not very fit and active.*
- *I don't do things with my kids.*
- *I'm the worst possible father!*

Positive cycle

The positive cycle on the other hand shows how we might react to a "mistake" more as an unexpected outcome, which we can use as food for thought and for creating new ways of approach and enhancing self-perception.

- *That nearly went in.*
- *My backhand's improving.*
- *I'm a reasonable player.*
- *I feel more fit and energetic.*
- *I bounce around with the kids.*
- *I really like myself now as a dad.*

Reinforcing the positive

Repeated affirmations help us to reinforce the positive cycle.

As early as 1913, Emile Coué, a pharmacist who had noted and used what later became known as the placebo effect, advocated repeating positive beliefs every day, in the belief that the repetition embedded a positive self-fulfilling prophecy and so helped build self-confidence, resourcefulness and performance. This method of autosuggestion, the Coué method, became very popular and widely adopted in both Europe and the USA. An example would be saying to yourself every day, *"Every day in every way I am getting better and better"*.

Though this format is simplistic, and the method has been questioned in the intervening century, it was perhaps the genesis of an idea which has been developed by others and has been incorporated into our wider cultural understanding. Many people find that positive affirmations and mantras are beneficial in promoting wellbeing. Research into the effects of positive thinking show that it helps us to maintain a resourceful and satisfied state of mind.

The strategies above are part of a process of self-compassion. We don't need to beat ourselves: we need to learn, be more accepting of our (past) selves and more able to grow and develop.

Chapter 3

Making connections

Making connections

The self is the starting point. If we don't know much about ourselves, we will find it hard to recognise or understand others' responses to us and their different needs. We may find working with them hard or mystifying. Now, we expand into exploring our communications and interconnections with others. We notice:

- How their views of us may differ from our views of self
- How the reverse is also true: we don't experience them in the same way that they see themselves
- That we all make assumptions and guesses about each other
- That we may expect others to react as we do
- How our best intentions may upset or confuse others

The fundamental thing here is the recognition that others *are* other. They may seem superficially like us or have had similar experiences or backgrounds: and they are still other. Their needs, wants, preferences and ways of processing are all subtly theirs. Understanding that, and remaining curious and interested about it, forms the basis of good relationships.

Beyond this, none of us is a single, simple, consistent self. We interact with numerous people for a variety of purposes and each person in the interchange is likely to bring different aspects of themselves to the interaction. This wide range of people each seem to require us to wear different hats: colleagues, line reports, teams, managers, customers, family, friends, networking groups, interest groups, society as a whole.

As we interact with each of these sets of people, we meet our own different needs and may contribute to some of theirs. These include collaboration, negotiation, mutual support, shared activity, fun, connection, love. Not all of these are appropriate for the work context!

This chapter offers several models which allow us to explore the different perspectives of pairs or groups of people as they interact. You'll probably find that one of these speaks to you more clearly than others. It doesn't matter how we describe and accept the otherness of people: just that we do. So try these approaches and see which works best for you as something to hold onto when interacting with colleagues and others.

Chapter 1 mentions António Guterres, UN Secretary General, saying in 2016, *"When two people are together, they are not two but six. What each one is, what each one thinks he or she is, and what each one thinks the other is"*. Several of the approaches here speak to this mix of how we perceive others and how they perceive us, the shadowy, often unrecognised figures in our interactions.

Frog versus prince/princess

You get what you focus on. We can all fall prey to self-fulfilling prophesies and pre-programming ourselves. If I approach a task thinking it is difficult and I am unlikely to succeed, that is probably what will happen.

This follows through into how we view others … and they us. We often know, without specific evidence or explanation, how others think of us and rate us. This is because we (and they) leak our feelings and responses. Responses which we think are hidden within us show up as "tells". The term tell comes originally from poker, used there to describe the unintentional signals a player gives about her hand, what she's feeling about it and how she may play it. The aim is, of course, to keep a "poker face" so that your opponents have no clues about your position. Psychologist Peter Collett describes, decodes and discusses the more everyday tells which we all exhibit in *"The Book of Tells"*. Essentially tells are tiny gestures and expressions which we hardly know we are exhibiting but which give others clues about our feelings, thoughts and responses.

Tells are very personal and their significance is individual so that we don't all signal the same thing by biting our bottom lip or tapping our left forefinger. These mini movements form a pattern in our behaviour which is very much our own and may include our own signature tell. These are often the things which enable mimics/impersonators to make themselves instantly recognisable as another person, even if they don't entirely look like that person: the tiny ticks and tells are taken in by the observers, who rapidly recognise who is being parodied. So, people imitating Donald Trump, for instance, emphasise small hands and a series of gestures including making a ring with thumb and forefinger. Homework! Watch some comedy shows!

Our assessment, prejudgements and prejudices about people seep through into our approaches to each other and may be visible and decodable through our tells. This is not just in the big generalised prejudgements but in our assessment of other individuals.

Imagine you turn a corner onto a corridor: just entering at the other end, is someone whom you don't rate, you don't want to exchange greetings with, you feel uncomfortable about. You walk along that long thin space towards them, making eye contact (or not) and wondering how fast you can get past and away. You exude some of these feelings. If as we turn that corner we see a frog, the other person is likely to feel froggy and respond in a froggy way (whatever that is!) and if we see a gorgeous star of a person and greet them accordingly they are likely to rise to that estimate … at least in that moment. We are constantly priming and programming each other.

Practise expecting and seeing the best in people. See what people can do (not what they can't); what they are good at (not their gaps); who they are at their best (not their worst); and trust them to do the same for you. Say the best about yourself and others to keep this living virtuous spiral going.

N.B. You might reverse the above if you are an anti-monarchist ranidaphobic! People notice something of the "*how I think of you*" in our demeanour, stance and communication and this then influences how they in their turn respond to us. See the different stages of the *Who/How Cone*.

Johari Window

In looking more at the juxtaposition of how we see ourselves and how others see us, a useful place to start is the well-established Johari Window because it acknowledges that other people have views of us, which we cannot necessarily see.

The Johari Window, created originally by Joseph Luft and Harrington Ingham, helps us to see what we reveal to the world, what we keep hidden from others and what we don't (yet) know about ourselves.

- Those aspects which both we and people we interact with know, are shown in the top left quadrant of the diagram: the public area.
- Top right are the aspects which are not known to us. Think 360° feedback, which can be a surprise to us!
- On the bottom left is the area of our secrets; things we know about ourselves but are unwilling or unable to present to the world.
- Finally, the bottom right is the home of the unconscious, which is not known either to us or to others.

The arrows in the diagram indicate the potential to expand the public area. The simple, clear Johari Window model allows us to identify different areas of perception about us. In the exploratory work you are doing as you read this, you are expanding the public area while reducing the blind spot.

Working with the Johari Window

Try this

Sketch out your own Johari Window. Consider some of the things you noted
about yourself as you read Chapter 2. Note them on Post-its and see where they
fit on the model. They may be in the private or the public area. For instance,
in the public area could be *"I am demanding of others"*, while the really
uncomfortable behavioural manifestation that *"She is never satisfied with our
performance"* may be in the blind spot. One quality may be like a prism reflecting
different lights from different perspectives. We see ourselves one way. Others see
us differently.

Take a little time to place some of the things you have been working with in one of
the quadrants. Clue … it's unlikely any of them will go in "The Unknown"!

You may also be able to include comments from previous diagnostics or 360 reports you have had, which were puzzling. They might have sat in the blind spot previously, but as you understand them, they move into another area. Some of the subliminal messages you receive from frogs/princes/princesses may also fit.

When you think that you have completed a full enough picture, sit back and give yourself time to reflect on the overview.

- What are the implications of this fresh view of yourself?
- What else might you like to find out?

Many of us will have been offered diagnostic processes at work which present an analysis of our strengths and development areas. There are numerous diagnostic tests, personality profiles and programmes which offer us reports on our qualities. These are developed through asking the participant to complete a questionnaire either online or with a skilled practitioner. People often find the output of these helpful in encapsulating how they process or present.

However, this type of analysis is based on the answers the individual has given, so they can be criticised as self-generative. Their output is revealing and thought provoking and organisations continue to offer them to employees. It is perhaps less common for individuals and organisation to fully exploit the analysis to support choiceful change, though some do so, using this as the starting point for a professional development or coaching programme. Of course, there is the risk that we might feel that the profile has validated us by recognising our preferences and then simply carry on as before, saying to ourselves, *"Yes, that's me"*.

To be offered a view from outside, we may also have had comments from 360° assessments which offer us a snapshot of how we may appear to colleagues. The key here is to remember that these views are indeed "how we may appear". If we can genuinely accept them as a perspective rather than the whole truth, they can be very useful. They are not an absolute: just a view from the other side of the skin. And they offer us the opportunity to accept that others see us differently. We then have more data to work with: how things seem to us, and how things seem to others. Neither view is the whole truth and neither completely wrong. Both merit comparison and reflection.

If you have had diagnostics or 360 reports, consider which bits of them will be useful as you explore the sectors of the Johari Window above.

Many people know the Johari model and find it useful in relationship work especially for introducing feedback. Teams and colleagues can use it as a base to acknowledge that we all have blind spots and that exchanging feedback is just information which can be helpful to understanding and choice. The second diagram is also useful to demonstrate the potential to extend the public area through feedback, coaching, learning and development and other supportive interventions.

Contradictory perspectives

As we begin to acknowledge our own views of self and the perspectives of others, it's helpful to look at the complex process of two sets of these varied perspectives colliding! This is often known as a conversation!

6/9 conversations

In all our interactions with others, not only does each person come from a different stance and bring different perspectives, but we each have different internal voices too. All of us always have a range of these different views within ourselves, balanced differently in response to different situations.

The last chapter looked at aspects of self-esteem and self-confidence, thinking about our own picture of ourselves and our place in the world. Of course, much of this picture is built up from our experience of interacting with others. We do not come into being wholly formed as individuals, although our genetic makeup is a strong influencer. We exist in a human landscape – our family, friends, work associates and the wider community. Our lives gain meaning in relationship to others. How we behave and how we evaluate our behaviour changes according to the people we are interacting with.

We expand our view of ourselves through taking in the view of others. Then we have food for thought.

Insights from transactional analysis

There are frameworks which help us notice, name and navigate the shifting patterns of interaction that show up in our work and personal relationships. We present differently to different people

There are all sorts of models for understanding these dynamics. One which acknowledges different aspects of ourselves which produce varying responses with other people and in different situations is Transactional Analysis (TA). It does just what it says on the tin … analyse the transaction (interchange or interaction) between people. The insights of TA seem to us to shed a light on how we are in ourselves, how we relate to other people and how our interaction with others triggers emotions and default positions.

TA has origins in the work of Eric Berne in the 1960s. It is a valuable way to explore, understand and explain the conversations, which we hold with ourselves and with others. It is used to develop effective interpersonal work and relationships in business, education, family life and therapeutic settings.

Parent, Adult, Child – Which voice is speaking?

Sometimes we behave in ways that we don't expect or which we wouldn't consciously choose. This may be because of triggers which sometimes lead us to behave in ways that we don't intend or necessarily feel very happy about.

TA offers us the idea that there are several ego states:

- Parent
- Adult
- Child

An ego state is a set of behaviours, thoughts and feelings which characterise how we interact with the world at a given time. Each has its roots in the past – often in behaviour that we have copied from those around us without our realising consciously what we are doing.

We are not always fixed in just one of these states; but rather move around between them, again often without realising that we are doing so. One pattern of behaviour may crop up for us more often than others. We may consciously decide to position ourselves in one ego state and find that we are actually reacting from another one in a totally different way. When that happens, we have often been highjacked by something simple that subconsciously reminds us of interactions from our childhood.

The three ego states are Parent, Adult and Child. However, not all parents behave the same way in all situations. Neither do all children. So, it's helpful to think of different subsets of Parent behaviour and different subsets of Child behaviour.

The simplified subdivision of the three ego states illustrated in our diagram opposite is derived from the functional diagrams developed by several TA writers, and in particular adapted from *Tactics* by Rosemary Napper and Trudi Newton.

Parent, Adult, Child

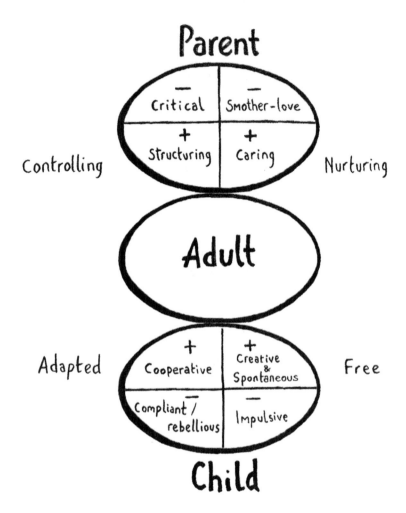

Here are some perspectives on the subdivisions.

Child. The Adapted Child ego state wants to please and appease or to avoid being controlled and so may be cooperative – or may be rebellious like a teenager, who bridles, denies and defends quickly. The Free Child is creative and wants to play. This too has both a plus and a minus side. The positive is spontaneity and the drawback is lack of grasp of both risks and consequences.

Parent. We probably all recognise the two Parent states: both may have the child's wellbeing at heart but the controlling one can find fault and be angry and … well, critical. While the nurturing one is caring, and (over) protective. This is where love may smother. Without boundaries set by the Controlling Parent, children grow up confused and without the necessary structure to help orientate their place in the world. Without nurturing love, children grow up with low self-esteem and forever battle to prove themselves worthy.

As the diagram and this explanation show, there are positive and negative sides to each of the Parent and Child ego states. They each carry emotional responses, which are not inevitably connected with the stimulus: they come only from our own preferences and patterns. That is, the situation doesn't in itself demand these emotional responses: they come from our own internal processes. So, for instance, when the boss, Deirdre, comes in shouting in a Controlling Parent state, different members of the team respond in different ways:

- Lee goes to a Compliant Adapted Child response *"Sorry Boss. I didn't notice. I'll stay late to sort it out"*
- Fred, also in a type of Adapted Child state, a more rebellious one, says *"Nothing to do with me. I can't help you there"*
- Luc has a Free Child response *"Well it's done now. Let's all go out for a drink!"*

Each of these reactions is common and understandable. It is likely that we each have a preference or default position which has its roots in our own world view, previous experience and filters.

Adult. Adult is the data place, objective, clear, calm; apparently not emotional … at least not carrying emotion that is not appropriate to the situation. At its best the Adult state keeps updating ideas, absorbing new information and developing new processes and strategies.

We all have the potential for each of the ego states within us and need them all to create an overall balanced response to circumstances. We may flip through the range of responses in a very short time finding our equilibrium.

Jaz

Jaz arrives at the station with only a short time till the train goes, to find there is no remaining parking space and thinks:

You should have left earlier.	Controlling Parent, critical
Oh dear, I've done it again. I should have learned better.	Adapted Child
Never mind. Poor you. Breathe.	Nurturing Parent
Hooray! Maybe I won't go to the meeting. I'll have the day off instead.	Free Child
OK. Where else can I park?	Adult

It's easy to recognise all those thoughts happening in moments as we adjust to the situation and manage ourselves to work with it. Few of us go straight to the final Adult thought without an emotional response. And this is fine. There is a balance of self-care and developmental criticism here which may help us avoid making the same mistake again.

What is not so healthy is if one ego state is so predominant that many of our responses are skewed. We have all met managers or leaders who are pretty stuck in one or the other of the Parent ego states.

Transactions

The exchange between Deirdre and Lee is an example of a transaction between a Controlling Parent and an Adapted Child. Lee is triggered by Deirdre's behaviour to respond in a habitual way. As this interaction perpetuates, Deirdre is repaid for shouting by Lee working harder and longer. Both become trapped in unproductive and ultimately damaging patterns.

Controlling Parent – Adapted Child

Relationships are stifled and stilted if they get stuck mainly in a pattern like the one in this diagram. There are other patterns of transactions in which people can be trapped. You may immediately have an instinct for where your default pattern is.

How likely are you to default to a particular ego state repeatedly with a particular person or type of person? Many of us apply what we would call our "head teacher syndrome" to people we cast as authority figures later in our lives. How often have we heard someone say of an admired or authority figure they'd anticipated meeting "*She was quite human really*"? Behind that throw away remark is the expectation that this figure will reduce me to Adapted Child. Or more accurately that I will respond in a Child state from my own interpretations and expectations.

Try this

Take a slice of time: the whole of a meeting or an afternoon's work and notice which ego state presented in your interactions. Either score it in some way or make a pie chart. When you can see a pattern, ask yourself if that was the most useful mix. Did it achieve the results you wanted? Did you feel how you would like to feel? How would you like to change the mix in the future?

- What did you notice?
- How useful was this pattern/mix?
- Did it achieve what you wanted?
- Did you feel how you hoped to feel?
- What might you like to change?

Try this

List significant people in your personal and professional life. This might include your life partner, parents, children, boss, peers at work, line reports, old friends and neighbours. Think about and jot down how you respond to them.

- Are you in Parent, Adult or Child?
- Is this consistent with each one?
- Are there patterns?
- What stands out for you?
- And how does this change your knowledge of yourself?

Person	P/A/C	Noticing and Learning

Where we find that we always have similar interactions in a particular relationship, we can look at what each of us is contributing to the mix, and what we are hooking in each other. We may be able to check with the other person what the pattern is, what assumptions it is based on and what choices we have for approaching conversations differently. At the very least we can notice our own responses and consciously choose to respond in other ways.

Think about what hooks you. In this sense a hook is something external which is interpreted by us in a repeat way and which pulls (hooks!) us into autopilot in our response. For instance, when called by our full name, rather than the usual abbreviation we may immediately default to Adapted Child because in early life the full form was used only when we were in trouble.

The hooking process

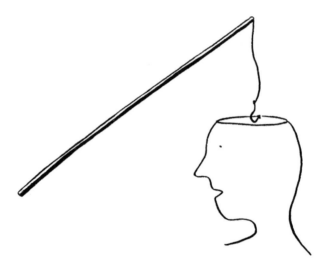

Even a casual question can hook an automatic response. We react like this, often at an emotional level as well as a cognitive one, because of an unquestioned assumption and this reaction may not be as useful as we would like, or it may not necessarily fit the circumstances. It is interference with an appropriate choice of response. If we were not hooked, we could pause to reflect. This could lead us to question underlying beliefs and where they might come from. Then we might be free to choose a more useful way forward, releasing our potential.

Recognising some of our default patterns or triggers is a useful stage in developing our understanding of ourselves. We might discover, for instance, that we default to a defensive posture when someone stands while we are seated; or are always slightly aggressive in a particular meeting; or react sharply when a person uses a word we don't know or quotes statistics (always remember that 84.73% of statistics are made up on the spot). We may feel cowed by a particular type of accent or a particular qualification.

If we are fully honest with ourselves, we will recognise that we can be hooked to make snap or stereotyped judgements about a number of things/people. Historically this has served our species well and has helped us to survive. When something with sharp horns charges towards us with its head down, we do not need to stop and think about our reaction and allow for the possibility that it may want to be stroked. We need to run and climb a tree. This quick (feels like instinctive) response serves us less well in many of today's complex interactions.

It's not helpful to make the same judgement about every person with an orange shirt, or a tattoo, or a short skirt, or green eyes or a beard. And this book does not explore the larger political and sociological field of prejudice. However, we all make prejudgements based on our experience and early programming. Often, we then have to spend a lot of time and effort later unpicking and recovering from our habitual judgement for example, that anyone with a loud voice intends to out-argue me!

Allow yourself some time to acknowledge what sorts of situations or people hook you into ineffective habitual or repeat responses. All this reflection helps us to move into self-knowledge and towards self-management.

It is ideal for much of our interaction at work to come from an Adult ego state. And that doesn't mean that we are not caring, thoughtful, strong and human. It just means we are not making an emotional meal of things which are facts and processes.

As we look at the attributes and apparently small things which may hook us, it's also worth considering what may stop us approaching each interaction openly, willing to accept the other person. There are numerous internal interferences. Before we even begin to talk to another person we may have developed a state which makes clear and purposeful communication unlikely. More of this in Chapter 5.

Scarcity and abundant thinking

Something else which might impact on the degree to which we can share and work creatively with others, is whether we have a pattern of scarcity or abundant thinking.

Scarcity thinking originates from experience of lack in other contexts or perhaps competitiveness, so our default view becomes *"There isn't enough to go round. We can't all have it. I can't get enough. I have to keep my work and plans secret to have any chance to gain what I need against the odds."*

This mindset is seen in many contexts and is almost always a sad waste of potential synergy, collaboration and mutual benefit.

The reverse of this is abundant thinking, which leads us to support others, share information and creativity, believe the whole is more than the sum of the parts and rejoice in shared success.

There are several strands of these theories about how we bring results onto ourselves by the view we take of the world. The law of attraction, for instance, has a long history which can be traced back to some early religious theories and which also resulted in hugely popular books like *Think and Grow Rich* by Napoleon Hill. Fundamentally the Law of Attraction suggests that if you focus fully on something, you attract it into your life. This theory has the obvious drawback that if I don't have the things I want, it is clearly my fault. Double whammy!

More accessible and acceptable to the twenty-first century intellect is the idea of *Growth Mindset*, proposed by Dr Carol Dweck. This body of work expounds the idea that our fundamental attributes are just the starting point. We can work on these and develop them as a foundation for achieving more and fulfilling our potential. A growth mindset is the opposite of a fixed mindset, which believes in innate limitations and settles for an initial estimate of what outcomes someone "like me" can achieve.

Strands of all these ideas come together in the concept of abundant thinking. Essentially the focus is on potential and growth, rather than lack and protectionism.

The growth of a new profession and market sector makes an interesting study of this. Taking the one we know best, coaching, we remember when the profession was very new. Almost no one had heard of it. Coaches were all trying to explain coaching to potential clients in order to create demand. Many adopted the view that they were in competition so they:

- Were wary of networking
- Didn't talk to other coaches
- Hid their ideas and methods
- Tried secretly to discover what others were up to.

Those who noticed that there were millions of potential customers who would benefit from coaching and only a very few coaches, shared ideas and supported each other. This paid off! For example, when a coach is working with one person in a business, other coaches will be needed to work with their colleagues, to avoid a conflict of interests. So, groupings of coaches call on each other to support a whole team or business. There are also huge gains in being able to call on a colleague with a different specialism or develop new approaches through talking to others in the same field.

If we, Sarah and Jenny, had adopted a scarcity mindset, we would not have agreed to share our thinking, would not have created new models which come from joint processing and would not have published and travelled widely working with coaches and leaders in many countries.

The belief that sharing and supporting pays off, leads us to introduce the idea of generosity in an emotional bank account.

The emotional bank account

Many people who explore their interactions with, and expectations of, others, have found a simple concept surprisingly powerful. It is the idea of the emotional bank account. It works exactly like a real bank account. Fundamentally, you can't draw out until you have paid in: you may in time be allowed an agreed overdraft and trouble ensues if you go over the allocated amount. You need to keep making payments if you want to withdraw. So, if you are new to an organisation you may be able early on to get your team to stay late and pull out all the stops in a difficult situation, but you won't be able to make that withdrawal from your account very often until you have built up some credit with them.

Here are some typical deposits and withdrawals:

Deposit	Withdrawal
Genuine and specific thanks	Demanding things
Positive feedback and praise	Not greeting people
Courtesy	Never asking how they are
Helping someone out	Ignoring them
Noticing how they are feeling	One-upmanship
Remembering things about them	Taking credit for their work
Sharing your chocolate (occasionally)	Keeping things for yourself (especially the chocolate)

Try this

Who is important to your working day?

Make a table of your bank balance with three colleagues.

- What do you notice?
- Who makes more deposits?

Colleague	Deposit	Withdrawal

- What might make things more balanced?
- What would you like to change or develop?

What about your neighbours? What behaviours might be deposits or withdrawals? Common elements for a balanced exchange include, noise levels; parking habits; reciprocal care when people are on holiday/ at work/ ill; invitations; borrowing.

Neighbour	Deposit	Withdrawal

We've all had neighbours who don't seem to pull their weight. When we reflect, we can probably see that the exchange was unbalanced. Most of us keep finely tuned reckonings internally, possibly without even realising we are doing it. Then the balance tips and we think, *"That's it"*. Or, *"He's gone too far"*.

It can serve us well to become more aware of these balance sheets and to review them so that we can make deposits appropriately or perhaps ask for things we need.

We can minimise the interference of a negative balance sheet by contributing more ourselves and/or becoming assertive about our needs.

Attitudinal shift

All these frameworks can help us to be more aware of our impact, make shifts in our approaches and improve our interactions and outcomes.

Frog/Prince/Princess is an example of this. When we choose to see someone in a different way, we offer both ourselves and them new possibilities for how to respond and interact with each other. If a manager does not believe that a report is capable of carrying out their job effectively, this tends to be a self-fulfilling prophesy. The converse is also true. A positive belief from the manager acts as a support and motivator to the colleague, who is then more likely to fulfil their potential.

And it's not just work relationships. If we truly believe someone is capable, that belief shines from us and they will usually live up to our estimate.

And if we believe we can, we can.

Here's some other examples of how we can shift how we see someone.

Name	Current Attitude	Shift
Cathy	New and inexperienced	Actually, been here 18 months and did a great job of work on that project.
Satu	Quiet mouse: nothing to say for herself	A thoughtful observer: may have useful insights: gets on with things.
Tunde	Grumpy and rude	Under a lot of pressure at home and work. Always delivers on time.

The example above of the change in attitude to Tunde springs from some work with a senior leader in a Human Resources role a few years ago.

She was finding her line manager grumpy and rude and noticed that she was responding to him like an offended aunt! When she chose to consider him from a compassionate place (and this word was a strong guiding principle for her in other areas of life) she found their relationship immediately smoother, and much less of her mental energy was occupied by resentment about the way he treated her.

The phrasing *"he treated her"* shows us how we often personalise something which is not ours. That was just how he was: it wasn't personal: it came from his unthinking response to the situation.

When we are able to stand back, see that things are not aimed at us and choose to shift our perception and approach, we are better resourced to work with people and to free our own emotional responses to be more creative. A fundamental belief for coaches is that the people they work with as clients are competent, resourceful and whole.

Try this

Take a moment to think around some of the people you work with regularly.

- How do you rate them?
- What's your deep-down response as you think of them?
- Is it true?
- Is it useful?

Then stop and consider what might be more realistic and more supportive.

Name	Current Attitude	Shift

Reflective shift

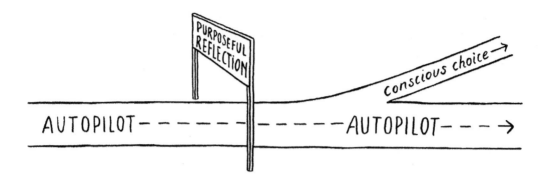

We often operate on autopilot. Somewhere much earlier in a relationship or our working pattern, we have adopted a belief which then becomes our operating instruction. Purposeful reflection can give us more conscious choice.

Giving ourselves time to reflect on what is happening in our conversations and interactions, gives us many more options and so feels resourceful and in control. This in turn helps us feel secure and able to manage our responses.

A starting point is that great question to self *"What happened then?"* or indeed *"What's happening here?"*. It slows us down and helps us observe and analyse a pattern of behaviour and then choose something different. To move towards a different exchange, reflect on:

- What are the patterns?
- What may be hooked in me which contributes to that?
- What's the outcome I want now?
- How can I manage myself differently?
- How do I now choose to approach this?

In short, engage brain before mouth! And know that most interactions are like a dance. If I change my step, you'll have to change yours. I can't actually change your behaviour directly, yet if I offer you a different stimulus you will probably change your response.

Linguistic shift

Language is a rich tool and many words carry a whole range of meaning and subtly different connotations for different people. There are one or two words in English which often set up adverse reactions (as there are in other languages) and which we can just stop using to good effect. This would create a linguistic shift.

But is an example. As soon as someone hears "but" come out of another person's mouth, they are alerted and ready to be corrected, challenged, overruled and told to do something differently. As a result, they often go onto the offensive themselves.

Mark: Please would you do X?

Sîan: But I'm doing Y.

Mark: You do what I tell you to do, when I tell you to do it.

But is a discount. It takes value from the statement that has preceded it and makes the following statement more important. It is a withdrawal from the emotional bank account.

Dilma: I'd like to be promoted …

Ivan: But you've got no line management experience

Nour: But you've got too much on your plate already

Ahmed: But you've no experience with budgets.

Here is a reframe, (of which there will be more in Chapter 5) using *and* as a starter. While it may be the truth that Dilma has no line management experience, it might be more empowering to reframe the response:

Dilma: I'd like to be promoted …

Ivan: Yes, **and** I notice that you would need to develop some line management experience. How might we do that?

Try this

How could you reframe the other two responses to Dilma?

Name	But …	And …
Nour	*"But you've got too much on your plate already"*	
Ahmed	*"But you've no experience with budgets"*	

In internal dialogue we often use *but* in a similar way, discounting our dreams and limiting our potential.

I'd like to be promoted …

- *But my face doesn't fit*
- *But I'm no good at interviews*
- *But I messed up at school*
- *But I got drunk at the Christmas party*

This is self-inflicted punishment, which we can change with a linguistic shift.

Try this

But	And
"But I've got too much on my plate"	
"But I've no experience of budgets"	
"But …"	
"But …"	

Again, in English *"why?"* may have a similarly repressive effect. We tend to experience "why" as implying, *"There was a better way. You should have done it differently. You were wrong"*. And as soon as the word emerges from someone's mouth we begin to react defensively. We may be thrown backwards into a childlike response, expecting criticism from a parent or teacher, and lose the more balanced perspective of the adult.

Don't worry this isn't a word by word analysis of the whole of the English language. Those two words, *but* and *why?* are the ones to use with extreme care or avoid altogether. N.B. substituting "however" for *"but"* doesn't count!

A more general language shift, which we can choose to make, is to use some of the words and expression of the other person. This is literally speaking their language. So, if someone says:

"Do you see what I mean?"

Don't reply:

"I hear what you say".

Use their words or some in the same reference area, in this case visual. Hearing the same sort of word come back to us makes us feel heard and accepted and allows us to explain more and create shared understanding. This is the linguistic building of empathy which helps us align and work well together.

There is more on linguistic adjustments in Chapter 4.

Behavioural shift

All the above lead to potential shifts of behaviour and they are perhaps more internal than shifts of stance, body language, actions and behaviour. All the changes we may decide to make come from real listening to others and to ourselves so that we can genuinely choose to stand in our own best understanding and strength and accept others as different and still competent, whole and resourceful.

When our body language is congruent with our speech because we neither need to strut our stuff to convince ourselves and others of our skills nor to humble and belittle ourselves to curry favour, we present as real and connected. So, notice when you or others say something which doesn't match your stance e.g., speaking positive words in a depressed tone or with drooping shoulders and downward glance.

Mixed messages

If you see someone pulling at their hair and grimacing while saying, "*It's all under control*", what do you believe? The body language or the words?

Congruent body language, what you see is what you get, is reassuring to others who don't have to struggle to decode mixed messages. It allows clean and clear exchanges and takes us back to the idea, mentioned in Chapter 2, that what people want most from their leaders is honesty. In this case, honesty of presentation.

In certain situations, it may be useful to explore and practice how we want to be. As we are promoted or move into new roles or functions (e.g., presenting at meetings or conferences), we benefit from deciding what stance and behaviour best fits the role we are now inhabiting. We can give ourselves prompts to maintain the presence we want or anchors to help us hold to it. These can be as simple as wearing a particular item of clothing (different from the everyday) to signal to ourselves that today I am the chair/president/speaker etc. This is part of a conscious (which soon becomes internalised) shift to a new style, perhaps a leadership style.

Another aspect of behaviour which puts credit in the emotional bank account is doing what we've said we will do and acting in alignment with the values which we propound. This builds trust in others and internal ease for ourselves and it generates a virtuous spiral of response.

Chapter 4

Hooks and humps

Hooks and humps

Now it's time to focus on growing ideas and building strategy for when the going gets tough. Some of the interferences in reaching our potential are within ourselves; some relationships seem fraught with difficulty despite our good intentions. Interferences pop up; things do not always go as planned. Despite knowing the theory, it seems that we need to keep learning the same lesson over and over again. Other people don't behave as we expect them to. We know that we are a work in progress and that learning is character forming – and we do not want to have our character formed! We're OK how we are already, thank you!

When things don't go as we intend, our resolve may crumble, and we may get hooked into old patterns which have previously led to unsuccessful outcomes. No single solution fits every challenge. There are however, tried and tested approaches which will have a positive impact on outcomes: how we feel, how we communicate and what we achieve. We will explore some of these in this chapter.

Limiting and undermining beliefs

When we have fixed beliefs about ourselves, we limit our potential. We tell ourselves unhelpful stories, as we have seen in Chapter 2, which in effect become self-fulfilling prophesies. As a result, we put boundaries around the possibilities that we see and shy away from challenges that we think we are not up to.

Our beliefs have their roots in what we learnt as children, absorbing the unwritten rules of the home as we watched how the adults around us interacted, as well as the verbal admonishments, myths and stories. Because these beliefs go back so far to the time of non-verbal memory, they become part of our very fabric.

The term "belief" covers many things. Different people's beliefs may include rules about what they ought to do, how they ought to interact with others, how society should be organised, how the world was created, what they as individuals are capable of. They may include beliefs about what girls/boys can do, what people who come from certain social groups are capable of, or how you need to behave in order to win love or approval.

Once a critical mass of people in the group surrounding us has a particular belief, it becomes almost part of the air we breathe, an unwritten rule about how to behave. Rules like this exert pressure to conform and guilt when we fail to do so and it can be difficult to question culturally-held norms openly. Once they are embedded deeply enough, they may seem impossible to change.

Many people see what they believe as the foundation of their being and the basis on which they interact with the world. They may say, "*That's what I believe. You can't change your beliefs*". They form their self-image in relation to the rules they have learnt, which could be liberating, but is more often limiting and can even be damaging.

A fixed belief limits what we expect of ourselves and others and all the rules about behaviour, which stem from a belief, give rise to judgement and criticism of both ourselves and others.

How could we think about beliefs differently?

There are two definitions of the word belief that we have found thought provoking. They are that a belief is:

1. A firm opinion, an acceptance of fact or statement
2. A principle accepted as true or real without proof.

Opinions can be changed. Fresh evidence may emerge which changes what we think. The principles on which we act may develop through the course of our lives as we accommodate fresh information and different experiences.

Beliefs give boundaries to our known world and make navigating it manageable. Yet it can be liberating to realise that we can choose to redraw our boundaries in the light of new knowledge and understanding. Beliefs do not have to be absolute, for ever. They can be provisional frameworks which can be tested, challenged and adapted in the face of fresh information.

It *is* possible to change our beliefs, alter the balance of different characteristics and get different outcomes in terms of feelings, behaviour and impact.

The first thing is to believe that it's possible to change. Maybe not to change everything, since we all have innate propensities and how we function in the world is always a combination of nature and nurture. We can however influence some of the way we think, feel, and show up in the world.

For example, the belief that we "ought" to be positive is very much part of contemporary culture in some parts of society.

There are many variations of the positive exhortation to believe in the possible, attributed to Henry Ford, "*If you think you can, you're right, if you think you can't you're right*" and later elaborated in self-help manual after self-help manual. The obligation to think positively may catch us in a double bind where we feel censured for our need to be honest or express difficult emotions and may become in itself a source of self-blame and paralysis.

We may end up saying

- "*I know I ought to…*"
- "*I should …*"
- "*I must …*"

and beating ourselves about the head for yet another failure.

The hooking process goes like this. Someone comes up to us and says, "How's business going?" We may feel insecure about how our business is going. When we hear the question, our insecurity is hooked. And we may have a belief that we should present a positive front all the time. So, we respond "It's all fine" without thinking. We suppress our inner anxiety. We don't evaluate or make a conscious choice about how to respond. In addition, we may have concluded previously that we appear weak and vulnerable if we talk about things going badly.

The belief that we all ought to be positive is one example of a limiting belief, which could lead us to respond on autopilot. Remember Jenny's story, described in Chapter 2. For Jenny, feeling uncheerful ▶ self-disgust ▶ lack of resourcefulness ▶ greater self-criticism. Surprising that she doesn't hit herself over the head with a hammer more often!

Another potentially undermining belief might be that we should be perfect in order to gain other people's approval. So, we try to win approval by appearing seamlessly good at everything we do, riding smoothly over every obstacle in our path. Our focus on the dual need for perfection and earning approval can be a huge interference to use our energy and skills to their full.

I must be perfect to gain approval ▶ ▶ ▶

▶ ▶ ▶ *I think about approval all the time* ▶ ▶ ▶

▶ ▶ ▶ *My attention is not fully on what I'm doing* ▶ ▶ ▶

▶ ▶ ▶ *I criticise myself for underachievement.*

Everyone is human, fallible and imperfect; a work in progress. We are learners together: and all the more likely to learn effectively, and help others learn too, when we are able to share the difficulties openly and discuss how to overcome them.

Try this

Make a list of all the messages you give yourself about what you *have* to do.

Then rewrite the messages using more provisional verb forms, and adding conditions:

- I might

- I could

- I can

- I chose to

- I'll consider

- I plan to

- I hope to

- It's possible to

- I'm opting for

- I'll find out about

- I'll experiment with

- I'll see what happens if

Exploring possibilities and giving ourselves a choice helps us to feel empowered and genuinely positive about the future.

Obligation	Possibility
I have to be positive about my hospital test	I could tell X how I'm really feeling
I must keep going or it will all fall apart	I could stop for a while and see what happens
I'm not allowed to say what I really feel	I might experiment with saying what it's like for me
Other people won't like me if I'm not smiling all the time	Maybe other people don't want to smile all the time either
	Not smiling all the time might help them to be more real

The examples above reveal beliefs about what we have to do in life. They are influenced by the world around us – our families, friends, colleagues, local community, cultural and national norms. Quite often these influences are outside our awareness and we adopt them without consciously choosing to do so.

Paying attention to the patterns of our thinking and what we say, can help us unpack these underlying beliefs and decide whether they are useful to us and we want to keep them or whether they limit us in some way and we would prefer to change them.

Can a leopard change its spots?

Many people are hooked by thinking that their beliefs are immutable and their character is a given. We might hear them saying, *"You can't change a leopard's spots"*, *"That's just me"*, *"That's just what I believe"*, *"I'm too old to … "*, *"People like me don't … "*. When they do this, they run the risk of setting themselves in stone, of becoming the immutable centre of their own universe. Not only might they have fixed beliefs about themselves, but this might also extend to how they think other people ought to relate to them.

Surjit, Maisie, Tom and Anita

Surjit was leading a small senior management team which was experiencing problems with communication. A lot was unsaid. Individuals in the team tended to dismiss each other's points of view and jumped to conclusions about what silences meant.

If Anita crossed her arms while Tom was talking, he interpreted it as rejection. When Tom tossed ideas around without much attachment to them, testing them out by hearing them come out of his mouth, Anita listened carefully, holding herself still so that she could think about what he was saying and could make up her own mind before she ventured her own opinion. With eyes down, she was silently intent.

Tom's rules said that you showed people respect by looking at them full in the face, smiling and nodding as they talked. He expressed his annoyance forcefully because he grew up in a family that believed in saying how they felt with no restraint.

Surjit felt out of control. He wanted everyone to work together in harmony to achieve the team objectives. He screwed up his face as he thought about this. Anita and Tom interpreted this as disapproval and became less interested in working together.

Maisie was new to the team and told the others how difficult it was to fit in. Tom and Anita said, *"That's just how we are. You'll get used to us. You can't expect us to change, you've just got to understand us and work with us how we are"*.

What is the outcome of thoughts like these? Mostly they stifle new thinking and block the possibility of change. What people get is what they've always got. And they get what they focus on.

What you get is what you've always got

Surjit's team decided to ask for external support to help them understand the differences in their preferred styles, so they could have greater insight into themselves. They learnt more about how other people perceived them and why they responded to each other as they did, triggered into knee-jerk reactions by certain behaviours.

With fresh and sometimes unexpected insights came choice. All four learnt to be more open and explain what was going on for them – and also to enquire more about how their behaviour impacted on the others. Diagnostic tools described later in this chapter give us a shorthand for understanding our preferences and differences and how we might adjust to others.

Bus stop bias

Because we live inside our own heads and our own thoughts are second nature to us, we sometimes assume that other people think like we do. Not so! Not only do people behave in a whole range of different ways, they also think differently, hold different values and have different preferences for communication.

Instant response

Try this

Try this exercise, to surface what you know versus what you assume.

Look at the image above and write some notes, accessing your gut reaction, about the people in it.

- What do you see?
- How might you approach this person?
- What do you notice about your own responses?

There have been numerous experiments over the years where the same C.V. is presented with a different picture or name attached and then a comparison is made of the number of interviews each variant receives. Sometimes the numbers differ vastly. Similarly, the same person presented differently (clothes, hair, etc.) will get very varying responses. The responses have their roots in the filters, beliefs, baggage, preferences or norms of the respondents and limit the potential for inclusive and fruitful interaction, development and synergy.

Adjusting to other people's preferences

If, in the interests of "fairness", we approach everyone in the same way, we are not likely to get the same response or achieve the same impact. That's because each of the people we interact with has their own filters, baggage and preferences. Learning how to adjust our responses and so our approach can be the key to working well with others and enjoying it!

"Why me?" you might say. *"Why should I be the one to change?"* The answer is, that the only person I have control over is myself. Changing how I behave changes the way other people perceive me and respond. It's a chain reaction! (see the *Who/How Cone* in Chapter 2). Experimenting can be fun.

There are lots of personality/behavioural assessment tools which can tell us something about tendencies and preferences. Some of them are used around the world, others more localised. One very well-known tool is Meyers Briggs Type Indicator® (MBTI®). Another is DISC. Both draw on Carl Jung's work on psychological types in the 1920s, in which he identified four personality functions, Thinking, Feeling, Sensation and Intuition, and also the additional lenses of Introverted and Extraverted preferences.

Working with a diagnostic assessment tool helps us recognise our own preferences, understand ourselves better, see why others may respond differently and think about how we might adjust our behaviour to have smoother working relationships. It gives us understanding and choices about how we work together. Because it is based on external data, it allows potential for joint adjustment without the interpretation of personal criticism. It's worth finding this shared language for groups, who want to acknowledge and accommodate difference in order to get the best from each member.

DISC

Building on Jung's work, William Marston described four behavioural styles, each with their own strong characteristics. These are often referred to as personality styles and relate to how much a person is outgoing or reserved and how much they are people orientated or task orientated.

The letters DISC refer to each of these four broad brush styles:

D = Drive – outgoing and task orientated

I = Influence – outgoing and people orientated

S = Steadiness – reserved and people orientated

C = Compliance – reserved and task orientated

While there are more conventional ways of describing each of the styles, Sarah developed her own set of images when working with a group of managers at a fruit and vegetable wholesaling company. The aim was for the managers to understand themselves and their own reactions better and develop ideas about how to get the most out of others.

In broad terms, the images relate to the preference types like this:

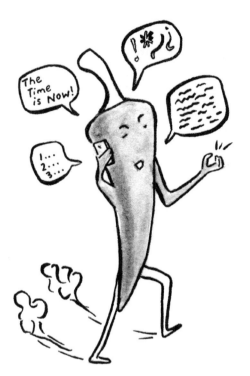

Ds as Red Hot Chilli Peppers: They are fast-paced, determined, pack a lot in. They tend to be optimistic, full of energy, strong-willed. They like strategy and control, ask challenging questions, are keen to sort problems out *now*. They may do something else while you are talking, interrupt you and run behind schedule because they have so much to do. Like chilli peppers, they are unsubtle, fiery and generate heat. They might be heard to say, *"Just get on and eat it!"*

Is as Passion Fruit: They are sociable and friendly, emotional, talkative, positive, full of energy and fast paced. They like being the centre of the group, are full of ideas, tell stories and are persuasive and influential. They don't like being pinned down. They may delay decisions that could be unpopular. Like passion fruit, they put out tendrils and intertwine with others. They have beautiful flowers and need a warm climate to produce their best fruit. They might be heard to say, *"Let's have fun!"*

Ss as Apples: They are relational, caring and concerned for others. They look before they leap and need time to change, preferring a smooth progression. They may hang onto the familiar, be possessive and find it hard to make up their minds. Patient and thoughtful, they are often good listeners, loyal, reliable, supportive and cooperative. Like apples, they are reliable, wholesome, connected to the traditions of the past. They might be heard to say, *"It's worked well so far – why go looking for something new?"*

Cs as Bunches of Grapes: They are cautious, analytical, systematic yet creative, patient, precise. They may follow rules but conceal their personal feelings, be defensive and focus in on detail rather than out on the big picture. Like a bunch of grapes, in the middle of the bunch, you lose sight of the whole. While each single grape may be perfect, one on its own is not enough – yet paying attention to the quality of each grape will lead to a great harvest and better wine. They might be heard to say, *"Let's look at the detail".*

These fruits are very different in nature. They thrive in different soil and different climates. They grow in different ways. What suits one does not suit another. They are all delicious in their own way and are equally valid. They are all distasteful to some people at times.

If red hot chilli peppers want to get the most out of other chilli peppers, they can probably behave in a way which is second nature to them. They don't need to think and adjust. They get on with it, without much thought. If, however, they want to get the most out of a bunch of grapes, they need to adjust their approach. Breathing red hot fire just will not do the trick.

We all deal most naturally with someone who is like us, or who is enough like us that we don't have to consciously work out a strategy for engagement. Yet life would be boring if every piece of fruit in the fruit bowl was the same or if we always had Brussels sprouts with every meal. Projects are better when different points of view are brought to bear, which means that sometimes we must think hard about how we engage with people who are not like us. It doesn't mean there's something wrong with them. Or with us, for that matter. It just means that they are different. Learning to be flexible and agile in our approach can be fun as well as useful.

Thinking about what sort of fruit your colleagues are, and adjusting your approach, might help you get over misunderstandings and miscommunication, get your point across clearly and get the best out of others.

Adjusting to a style which is not our first preference can be a strain at times, so we need to be alert to potential stresses and develop strategies to take care of ourselves. We are likely to need different strategies for this with different types of people.

Try this

To get your point across clearly and get the best out of a red-hot chilli pepper (**D**):

- Be brief, direct, logical, facts and results orientated. Avoid telling them what to do, presenting problems, rambling, repetitions and generalisations.

To take care of yourself when working with a chilli pepper:

- See yourself as equal; be clear about focus and boundaries; prepare evidence in advance; know what your bottom line will be in negotiation; rehearse a clear message. Seek social relationships, eye contact and validation elsewhere.

To get your point across clearly and get the best out of a passion fruit (**I**):

- Be friendly, creating time to talk, collaborating, listening well, giving praise, helping transform ideas to plans. Avoid emphasising rules and regulations, giving them repetitive tasks, or long drawn-out projects.

To take care of yourself when working with a passion fruit:

- Allow time for positive social meetings; negotiate goals and build emotional engagement, ensuring that you have clarity about the outcomes of the work, and putting adequate support in place for getting the detail right. Record what you've agreed.

To get your point across clearly and get the best out of an apple (**S**):

- Show a sincere interest in them as people, giving them time to prepare and time to adjust, explaining roles and projects clearly, highlighting benefits over risks, encouraging. Avoid direct confrontation, going too fast, creating sudden changes, putting them on the spot, pulling rank.

To take care of yourself when working with an apple:

- Relax; allow time in your schedule to build relationship and clarity; remember that reliability and loyalty are invaluable. If you are more of a chilli pepper yourself, find other outlets for your heat and pace.

To get your point across clearly and get the best out of a bunch of grapes (**C**):

- Give them detail and specifics, autonomy, security, explanation, reassurance, time to prepare. Paint the big picture. Listen. Avoid off-the-cuff casual remarks, vagueness, pressure to meet deadlines, sudden surprises, bluntness and disagreement.

To take care of yourself when working with a bunch of grapes:

- Relax; allow time for building clarity, remembering that attention to detail reduces risk. Prepare for meetings so you too have facts at your fingertips and are ready for penetrating questions. Find someone else to support reaching deadlines.

Now MBTI®

Sometimes we typecast people as "difficult" simply because we don't understand them, and they behave in a way that does not match our expectations or preferences. Myers–Briggs Type Indicator® (MBTI®) is one of the best known of the many profiling tools which help people to identify broad behavioural preferences, and to think about how they differ from others.

So, here's a bit about MBTI® and how differences may show up in some situations.

The Myers-Briggs Type Indicator® (MBTI®) is so widely used that the combinations of letters used to describe a cluster of preferences have become a sort of shorthand for indicating a "type" and also what to expect of colleagues. Maybe you have heard someone say, *"She's very T"* or, *"I'm a borderline S"* as though this explains everything about a person. Or more helpfully, *"You seem to be in your E and my I can't cope! Give me a moment to catch up"*. This could be more productive than, *"Don't interrupt me!"* or, *"You don't listen"*, or, *"I don't know what you're talking about"*.

It's important to remember that MBTI® profiling, as other tools, describes behavioural tendencies rather than fixed ways of being. MBTI®, DISC and many other tools illuminate the way that people behave. They do not prescribe the future.

The MBTI® questionnaire helps to identify preferences in four distinct aspects of your personality.

There are 16 different "types" altogether, each one indicating something about:

- Where they prefer to draw their energy (E or I)
- The kind of information they prefer to gather or trust (S or N)
- The process they might use when reaching decisions (T or F)
- How they prefer to deal with the world around them (J or P)

In sticky situations people often operate from a place of comfort, where they can work within their preferred style rather than another more unfamiliar one. However, personality preferences are not cast in stone for ever, and people learn how to operate effectively in other ways as a result of experience, feedback and the prevailing work or societal culture.

If all the members of the team have an MBTI® profile *and* there is agreement to share what that profile is, you can all use the information to work out how best to adjust your approach to get the most out of working with that colleague. An agile leader can learn to respond in diverse ways to different people.

Now for a brief overview of what the different letters in a profile might indicate to us.

P likes to walk all the way round the problem, looking at lots of different aspects and possibilities.

J likes to reach a conclusion quickly, establishing a timeline of action and diminishing uncertainty as rapidly as possible.

F likes to take values and personalities into account, making adjustments in order to keep harmony.

T is focused on principles, logic and consequences.

S will want to discuss specifics and what's been done already.

N goes for the big picture.

E will gain energy from interaction with other people and may think aloud, speaking out before they have fully thought something through.

I will gain energy from thinking things through on their own and may like to have a good chunk of time to take in new information and work it through.

If you are intrigued by this very light touch introduction to MBTI® and personality preferences and want to explore more fully, perhaps start by reading some of the references at the end of the book and maybe follow up by training to be a qualified practitioner. In the meantime, here are a couple of broad-brush examples to consider.

People with different preferences approach problem solving in contrasting ways. This can be surprising if you assume that everyone approaches problems and life in general like you do and insisting on one style alone can alienate some of the people you work with.

Finding a solution with Sophia, an SFP

Imagine you have Sophia as a colleague in a crucial problem-solving role alongside you. You just want to get to the answer quickly and have done with uncertainty. Sophia however has a P in her MBTI® profile. P likes to walk all the way round the issue, looking at lots of aspects and possibilities. As she also has S in her profile, she will want facts and specifics as well. Add F to the mix and you can guess that she also wants to consider values and the impact on people. Challenge (SFPs) too much, by insisting on a framework of immutable policies and rigid timescales, and they will lose their motivation. The interference will be too great for them to achieve their potential – or indeed for the team to do so, since they will pull away from the collaborative effort.

- To align with her preferences and behave in a way she might like, be open to discussing all aspects of the problem, giving detail and considering group harmony.
- To stretch her, ask her to consider questions about timetables, scheduling and logic.

Flexing your behaviour to respect other people's preferences so that they feel their contribution is both valid and valued, builds trust, a necessary pre-condition for constructive challenge, which in turn helps people to see things in a fresh light and to achieve more both individually and collectively.

Getting the balance right helps everyone to achieve their potential.

In our experience, working with diagnostics for a whole team has many benefits. There is a shared way of classifying and understanding different thinking styles and behavioural approaches. This supports open discussion about contrast (and sometimes conflict) of approach and glitches in communication without personalised judgement and blame.

Persuading Nat, an NT

Now imagine you have to influence Nat, a rather vocal member of the team, who has the potential to derail a project you are leading. You want to influence Nat and bring him round to your way of thinking. He has a T in his MBTI® profile. T is focused on principles, logic and consequences and will like to get to the point. Add an N into the mix and you have someone who has a preference for long term strategy, connecting systems and models.

Whatever your own preference, talking about the atypical circumstances of the different people who might be impacted and the need to flex as you go, just will not work with a NAT. Nor will brainstorming with no practical outcome. These are distractions which could undermine the potential for you both to combine your different approaches in a complementary way to achieve better outcomes.

- Instead, talk about strategy and how an idea aligns with it.
- Offer evidence as the basis for debate.
- Show long-term implications and benefits.

Linguistic adjustments

You don't need a personality or behavioural report to notice that people have very different ways of expressing themselves. Sometimes these indicate preferences for particular senses, or filters for their understanding of the world, other times they are a product of the environment in which someone works or has been brought up.

Sales people are sometimes trained to be ultra-sensitive to the sort of vocabulary that someone is using so that they can adjust their own language to be more like the customer's. The theory is that if you use similar words and turns of phrase, the other person thinks you see the world in the same way as they do. They feel understood and give you trust. This in turn could be a good way of opening the door to a potential sale.

Coaches listen in a similar way and may adjust their language to be more like their client's language. The aim here is to align themselves to the client's way of thinking, to gain understanding, to speak in a way which is more easily accessible. This is a good foundation for trust and rapport.

It's a technique that anyone can use to make for more elegant communication and to build relationships.

Here's the sort of thing that people listen for:

- *Imagery.* Which of the senses does this draw on? Visual, auditory, kinaesthetic, olfactory or gustatory?
- *Cultural references.* What are the influences at play?
- *Thinking* versus *feeling* words
- *Pace* and *tone* of voice.

And here's some examples of the sort of adjustments you might make to improve your communication.

- If someone says, *"The picture's fuzzy"*, try asking *"What could bring it into focus?"*

- If someone says, *"That really doesn't ring true"*, try asking *"So how does it sound, then?"*

- If someone says, *"That feels like a step too far"*, try asking *"What would feel a better distance?"*

- If someone says, *"That smells fishy"*, try asking *"What would make it smell different?"*

- If someone says, *"That was disgusting. I had a bad taste for ages"*, try asking *"And if it had been really delicious. ... ?"*

In each of these examples, adjusting to use similar language is likely to open up thinking and exploration.

When language is very dissimilar, people may feel misunderstood, excluded, different and defensive. It costs nothing to tweak your imagery. It may feel clunky of course, if you use vocabulary and images which are not your norm but can lead to enhanced understanding and closer relationships.

Mismatched communication

A safe way to ensure the other person feels you are "speaking their language" is to do just that! *Use some of their words.*

This can be especially useful if you want to ask someone a question either to understand more fully yourself what they are saying or to get them to expand their ideas so that you can build on them together.

Try this

To shift linguistically, use the *Question Recipe*

- No more than seven words
- Contains between one and three of the other person's words
- Begins with *What* (or just possibly *How*)

As an example, Tez talks for a while about current tasks then says, "*I'm wondering how to approach the sessional report*".

Possible responses using the question recipe are:

- "*What works best for the sessional report?*"
- "*What's useful in the sessional report?*"
- "*What approaches work best for you?*"
- "*How would you like to approach it?*"

Often, we can use people's words back to them until we feel quite silly and self-conscious and they don't notice at all because we are echoing their thought process. Watch point … people do however know if we are not doing it in good faith. We must ask the questions with a genuine desire to understand, make progress and develop connection.

Sometimes we can move a stage further in adopting the language of the other by using a word or concept which is part of their preferred vocabulary or area of expertise but which they haven't just used in this conversation.

Brett

Brett, a finance director, was talking about difficulties in his relationship with his teenage daughter. There were several dead ends as he tried to use the vocabulary of psychology or what he understood as touchy/feely language.

When his coach asked him, *"How would you audit the relationship?"*, his demeanour changed, he got out a pen and started scribbling and drawing a rough chart. Further questions about risk areas and possible strategies followed. He genuinely saw the interactions differently at the end of the conversation and had both insight and a plan for new approaches.

The word "audit", so familiar and empowering, unlocked his thinking.

If the person you are trying to collaborate with or influence likes data, graphs and factual language – use data graphs and factual language yourself. Look at the evidence together, either on paper, maybe between you on a table, where you can point to facts that you want to highlight, or on a screen, with a way of pointing to different areas of focus. Avoid "feeling" language. Say *"I think"*, *"this leads to"*, *"the basis for this is … "*. Be glad when you get recognition of your process.

If the person you are trying to collaborate with or influence likes feelings, generalisations and encouragement, adjust your language accordingly. Be aware that much of the meaning may be conveyed by tone and body language as well as simply vocabulary. Give eye contact, smile, repeat back what you've heard that's gone well. Give reinforcement, validation and praise.

Feedback and praise

When people are offered feedback, they may have an automatic recoil, expecting negative criticism. Feedback can be positive too! We all need feedback on how we are doing and we especially need an energising mix of positive validation and developmental suggestions/instructions.

Useful feedback is:

Contracted for	Agreed in terms of purpose, focus, desirability, use
Focused	Relates to purpose, criteria, context; gives relevant information
Purposeful	Links to a positive goal, good intentions; creates steps for action
Strength centred	Based on belief in individual potential; uses strengths as springboard
Objective	Based on observed evidence; direct;
Specific	Gives detail in terms of actions and impact observed
Constructive	Maintains positive emotional state; based on support and goodwill
Non-judgemental	Context of no-blame culture; mistakes are opportunities for learning
Time sensitive	Given at as soon as possible, while still relevant
Praise weighted	Ratio of praise to development points – 5:1. Finishes with a positive.
Truthful	Honest. Unadorned with pretty phrases. May be sensitively phrased
Elicited	Coaxed out of person observed if possible
Confidential	Unless otherwise agreed explicitly in advance

Praise the SIGA way

Use the acronym SIGA to prompt you if you have problems working out what sort of praise might work best.

S = Specific
I = Immediate
G = Genuine
A = Appropriate

Specific praise lets you know precisely what it is that you have done right and why it has been a good thing to do. Knowing this, you can do it again and leap even further forward.

- *"I really liked the way you completed that report. It was succinct, well-laid out and highlighted the key points".*
- *"It was great that you asked Dev what he thought. He'd not been contributing until then and he took a much more active role after you included him".*

Immediate praise is most effective. It encourages us and others to continue with the behaviour being praised. It's recent so that we can remember it easily/fully and know what it felt like to work/behave that way. Immediacy also makes praise more believable. If we wait too long to congratulate people, what we say may lose its emotional impact, as the praise is detached from the action. Praise that is too late can be counterproductive.

Genuine praise, given with a smile, a direct look and an appropriate tone of voice, warms the cockles of our hearts. Deep down, everyone likes being praised, although we may be suspicious if we feel the person praising us is not sincere or wants to manipulate us in some way.

Appropriate praise is the right amount of praise for person and the situation. Too little praise results in people not feeling cared for or not knowing if they have done the right thing. Result – demotivation. Too much praise is also inappropriate.

Going into ecstasies over someone behaving well when doing something which isn't a challenge for them; praising a soggy cake to the skies, when it might be more appropriate to praise the effort, the thought, the first stages towards being a great cake maker; exaggerating what one person has achieved to give an example to someone else – these things simply do not work. They undervalue the act of praising and, in a funny way, undervalue the action that we have praised. We need to get the right degree of praise for the action, the person and the context.

Appreciation of work well done is one of the greatest motivators.

Catch them doing well – and let them know!

Dog training for humans

Think about dog training: the dog is offered masses of positive reinforcement of good behaviour: two of the basic tenets of dog training are:

- Training should be based on *positive* rewards.
- *Never* punish your dog – this will cause it to be frightened of you.

Pretty much the same applies to us. We need positive reinforcement and calm, factual correction or redirection.

Direct or delegate? Flexing leadership style

A couple more frameworks might help us reflect on how different people are and how to adapt our approach to work with them more effectively.

The first relates to our style of leadership and how much we instruct, at one end of the scale, or delegate, at the other. It's not productive to tell a highly skilled and motivated colleague the minutiae of how you expect them to complete a task. Nor does it lead to a great outcome if you throw a complex problem at an apprentice with no guidelines. Relationships and productivity are both likely to suffer. Flexing your style, considering the levels of skill and motivation of your colleague, is likely to lead to better outcomes all round.

Leadership style, skill and will

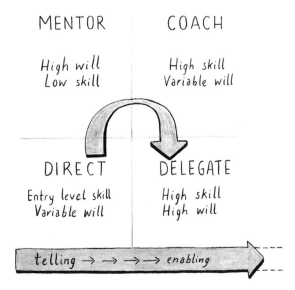

This diagram adapts the Situational Leadership model, which originates in the work of Hersey and Blanchard. It is appropriate to:

- **Direct**, if your colleague has entry-level skill, with varying degrees of motivation. Give clear instructions, and make boundaries, roles and responsibilities explicit.
- **Mentor**, if your colleague has low levels of skill or is transferring to a new area of responsibility, and at the same time has high levels of motivation. Guide and advise, drawing on your own experience and expertise.
- **Coach**, if your colleague has high levels of skill but is rather up and down in motivation, energy or confidence. Show you believe in their potential, ask open questions, encourage them to identify their own best way forward.
- **Delegate**, if your colleague is both highly skilled and highly motivated. Establish clear parameters within which they have freedom to operate. Encourage them to set success criteria, milestones and review points and to identify any support they need.

Inherited patterns

Sometimes the habitual way we react to others does not help either us or them to move forward. Many people learn patterns of behaviour as small children from observing their parents. We pick up carers' habits almost by osmosis, without analysis or choice, because that is just the way that adults around us behave. Generally, these habits seem to have a pay back – that is, they benefit us in one way or another. There is no blame attached to copying them ourselves in the first instance. However, later in life we may realise that we are caught in a repeating pattern which does not serve us as we might like. We might want to break out and think and behave in a more productive way.

The good thing is, these patterns are so widespread that psychologists and others have described them in models which help us to understand ourselves and to make conscious choices about how else to behave.

The Drama Triangle

The Drama Triangle is a model which helps to clarify the roles we tend to fall into when interacting with others. Developed by Karpman (1968), it describes three characteristic positions, each of which sees us replaying ineffective patterns of thought and behaviour. We may tend to take up one particular position more than another but may also move around different positions with different people in different contexts. When we take a position, we may be responding to a hook from someone else and we in turn may behave in a way that hooks others.

R = Rescuer

P = Persecutor

V = Victim

The Drama Triangle

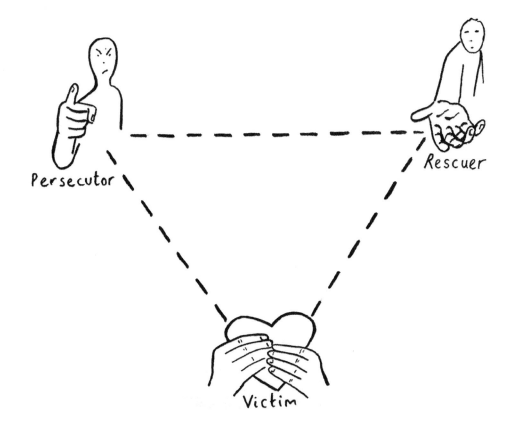

If we have a propensity to take on the role of Rescuer, we may be hooked by someone who says that they are overloaded and cannot manage and who simultaneously tells us how they admire our strength and skill. Our self-image is bolstered by the praise; in just a trice we see ourselves as stronger. At the same time, our best instincts come into play. We want to help someone who is weaker. We offer to take some of the load. We are hooked.

What's wrong with helping others, you might ask? Of course, there is nothing wrong with wanting to help other people when we have the capacity to do so. The problem comes when we fall so automatically into this pattern of helping that it becomes a knee-jerk reaction, distracts us from key priorities and disempowers the person we help.

This person may be caught in a learned pattern of helplessness. She may have learnt that when she says that work is just too much, someone steps in to help her out and she can do less herself. While help is often benign, an automatic default to helplessness stops us growing and assuming our own responsibilities. A repeating pattern of asking for help can trap us in a mindset where we not only think we are incapable, but also blame others for making unacceptable demands on us.

There are patterns of mind and thought that go with all three of the positions in the Drama Triangle.

Someone who is playing the role of Rescuer may:

- Think they are responsible for everything and as others can't manage, they have to step in and help.
- Say, *"I'll do that for you – Don't worry about me"*.
- Feel righteous and overburdened.

Someone who is playing the role of Victim may:

- Think that it is all too much, that this sort of thing keeps happening to them and that nothing can help.
- Say, *"I've got so much on, you can't expect me to do this, there's not enough time"*, *"You're so good at it"* and *"The system makes this all impossible for me – it's easier for him though"*.
- Feel full of fear and self-pity, singled out for unjust treatment.

Someone who is playing the role of Persecutor may:

- Think that they need to correct or realign other people who are weaker links in the chain and keep making excuses.
- Be convinced that someone is to blame and say, *"Whose fault is it that this isn't done?"*, *"When are you going to do it then?"*
- Feel threatened and pressured – and also right!

The Winners' Triangle

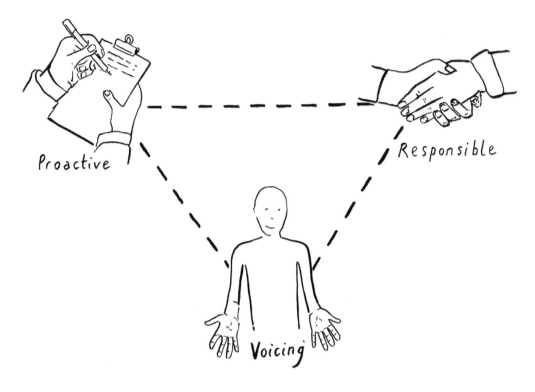

The good news is that there are ways out of these patterns. The Winners' Triangle, described by Choy, offers us alternatives.

R = Responsible

P = Proactive

V = Voicing

In our diagram:

- Responsible offers us an alternative to the Rescuer role
- Proactive offers us an alternative to the Persecutor role
- Voicing offers us an alternative to the Victim role

Move to Responsible

To move from Rescuer to Responsible, try this shift:

- **Think** that you are not responsible for it all; –you can choose what you do. Both you and others have boundaried roles and you can each assume responsibility for your part.
- **Say**, *"OK. So, this is what I hear you saying. And this is what we agreed. What I can do is this … How can we manage the rest of it?"*

Then hopefully you will feel empathetic, secure and strong.

Move to Proactive

To move from Persecutor to Proactive, try this shift:

- **Think** that everyone makes mistakes and having support to learn from mistakes helps us to develop. Think about adjustments that you could make and how you might find a way forward together.
- **Say**, *"How can we use the learning from this for the future?" "We can make this manageable together. What's your view of when and how we could do this?"*

Then hopefully you will feel lighter, encouraging and encouraged.

Move to Voicing

To move from Victim to Voicing, try this shift:

- **Think** that you could just be overreacting and there might be a different way of looking at things. Believe that you can say *no* if you want to and that you just may not need to do everything.
- **Say**, *"This is how I feel about it now – and I'd like to check a few things out by talking it through with someone else", "I need a bit more time and I could try out a few different things – and if they don't work, I could try something else".*

Then hopefully you will feel more self-accepting, interested in what might happen and experimental.

More inherited patterns

Many learned behaviours have their roots in our early childhood experiences.

Niamh

Niamh was working in a small company in a senior position. Her boss, Jai, had a strong agenda about the way the organisation should be run and a hierarchical view of leadership. When Niamh put forward an opinion in meetings, Jai often said, *"I'm going to stop you there"*, or *"You've had your time"* or *"I don't want ideas"*.

Niamh seethed inwardly. She felt shut down and as though her opinion didn't matter. Once she replied, *"I know you don't want me to finish"*. Another time she said, *"Are you telling me not to speak?"* Neither of these responses improved the relationship or made the meeting more productive!

A chance conversation helped Niamh to reflect on why Jai's comments struck such a raw nerve for her. Niamh was talking to another colleague, Kef, about growing up. She described what happened when as a child she had challenged a decision or point of view at the meal table. Her mother had sent her away to her room. Unable to put forward an opinion, she had felt disempowered, exiled and invalid. Kef asked what light this shed on how Niamh showed up at work.

And the light came on! At some subconscious level, when someone in power prevented her from speaking in a group, she was thrown back into a feeling of childlike powerlessness. It was difficult to draw on her strengths and take her place as an adult with an equally valid point of view.

This new awareness was the key to a change of behaviour going forward. Niamh learned to stand her ground calmly without being highjacked by emotion from the past.

Try this

Think back to your time as a child.

- What was your position in the family? Were you a first child? Middle? Last? Only child?

- What was your role in relation to other significant people in your family group? Were you an organiser? Rebel? Thought leader? Harmoniser?

- What were the rules in your family? The unspoken values?

- How did you learn to behave in order to survive and thrive?

- What are the stories you tell yourself and others about this period of time?

Now think about how you tend to behave in groups and teams at work.

- How much have the patterns of the past formed the person you are now?

- How useful are your learned behaviours in your current context?

- What alternative behaviours might be more appropriate?

- What support might you need to experiment with new behaviours?

Seeing yourself differently

Awareness is the first step towards choice and change. The patterns of the past are well established. At the same time, our brains have plasticity and with practice we can grow new patterns.

We sometimes use the analogy of choosing a country road in preference to a motorway. When you get on a motorway, you don't need to think too much about where you're going. You drive down a one-directional slip road onto the motorway. It's wide. The junction signs are huge. You don't need to change gear much. You don't need a map. The car more or less drives itself. After a while though, you may become aware that all you see is grey road and miles of metal. You might be caught up in the pace of other drivers and push yourself more than is comfortable or safe. You might lose sight of the countryside through which you are rushing.

Then maybe you choose to take a country route instead. You plan ahead, noticing where you need to turn. At first, you are hesitant because you need to consult your map frequently. There's more thinking when you want to overtake. Sometimes it's slow or the route is winding. With time, taking the country route becomes more comfortable and you start to take in the scenery. Changes in contour, trees, fields. Then it becomes second nature.

Building a new habit follows a similar trajectory. We behave in a habitual way, which we do not have to think about. Then we become aware that there is something unchosen about this habit and we look for alternatives. We make a choice to do something other. At first, we need to think a lot. The new habit is conscious and may be uncomfortable. With practice, the new neural pathways strengthen and the old pathways atrophy. Eventually the chosen behaviour becomes the new habit.

Once we are aware of being hooked to behave in a way that does not serve us well, we can think about how we would prefer to behave instead. For example, it may be that you realise that in a group situation you tend to fall silent and conceal your inner thoughts, suppressing your emotions as you do so; yet in a one to one situation you have learnt to be articulate and open about what you are thinking.

Try this

- Think about a group where you do not behave as you would ideally like to behave.
- Draw a sketch of the group including yourself, as a collection of stick people.

Now

- Notice where you have placed yourself and others and the stick people's relative size.
- Notice what you are feeling in your body as you look at your sketch.

Now

- Think about someone you relate to easily, with whom you can talk openly and exchange ideas on an equal basis.
- Draw a sketch of this two-some as a couple of stick people.

Finally

- Notice how you have drawn the stance of the people and the relative size.
- Notice what you are feeling in your body as you look at this sketch.

Knowing how you felt physically as you looked at the group sketch is useful because it is an indicator of being hooked. That sort of feeling coming on in a meeting is like an alarm – a sign that the hook is dangling, and we need to take avoidance tactics and consciously steer ourselves in a different direction.

Try this

Now try this to build an alternative choice of behaviour:

- Visualise yourself as vividly as possible in your preferred size and stance.

- Imagine yourself speaking strongly and calmly in an equal and open way.

- At the same time, make a physical gesture such as clasping your hands firmly, which you can connect to the feeling of being equal and calm. This gesture anchors your feeling for the future.

- Breathe.

- Practice the visualisation, the gesture and the calm breathing until you can quickly move from a state of agitation to a state of calm equality.

- Put your gesture into action whenever you notice the hook making its appearance.

Chapter 5

Ducking, diving and thriving

Ducking, diving and thriving

With the best will in the world, shit happens. There are conflicts and challenges in every size and type of community – small firms, large organisations, voluntary groups and families. Most people involved usually feel miserable, trapped and disempowered. Discussions are difficult, angry and seem to be going nowhere.

When we are well resourced, we can take a step back and weigh up the apparent shit, distinguishing between what would be hard for anyone to deal with and what we might be making worse because of our interpretation of events. We see patterns in the dynamics of the relationships and work out strategies to respond. We identify key issues and separate them out, giving them priority.

However, when the going gets tough, particularly at a time when we are already stretched thin, we are often so deeply mired in our feelings that we can't either get a perspective or manage the challenge. We need help to find different ways of looking at things, externalise and objectivise the conflict, be more resourceful and move forward.

There are many types of shit:

- Accidental shit
- Unintentional shit
- Situational shit
- Perceived shit
- Well-meaning shit
- Cultural shit
  … etc. … etc.

Most of these are not really a personal attack on us, even though that's how we might interpret them initially. The sharp, uncomfortable reaction, which we experience may belong to the role rather than the person: to the Chair of the Board, not Mae Hill. To the Head of Ops., not Jem Cohen. To the Receptionist, not Jack Ng.

So, first, STOP and wait. Give yourself a moment to know that this shit doesn't necessarily belong to you. Where we start from, and how we start, as we move to resolve a situation, are both vital to the outcome.

People frequently ask for tips on how to deal with difficult colleagues, difficult managers, difficult customers, difficult students, difficult staff. These are not real categories: people just behave how they behave and we have a choice of response. When we start out seeing people as difficult, it limits our power, range of options and choices (as you might remember from the story of the Frog and Prince/ Princess in Chapter 3).

If, on the other hand, we are able to view everyone (including ourselves) with compassion, then what might this unlock?

If we knew that we were doing:

- The best we could at the time
- The best we could with the resources available
- The best we could with the information we had

… what would be possible?

And if it wasn't a personal attack, what then? If this wasn't about us, but instead a reaction to the role that is currently and coincidentally ours, such as Head of Department (currently and coincidentally our role) what difference would that make to our reaction?

When a fly lands on our food, we often personalise our annoyance and upset offering interpretations like

- *There's a horrible fly on **my** food.*

The fly is just doing what flies do really well: it's a really efficient and effective fly, a useful part of the cycle of life. It doesn't know about food ownership!

So, when the going gets tough, PAUSE and notice it's like a fly. Pause and think about the desired outcome. Pause and know it's generally not personal. Pause and centre yourself. You are you and this is just the weather on the streets today (also not personal!).

Stories we tell ourselves ... again!

Telling yourself that the fly is doing what it does best in the circumstances is a reframe of the situation, so the personal attack story loses power. It's an example of reframing our interpretation of what's going on, of retelling our story, so we have a way of thinking, which frees us for action. The stories we tell ourselves may make or break our ability to surmount the difficulty. Stories include our interpretations of the situation, our imaginings about what's going on, our assumptions about what other people think and believe. And we can change those stories.

We may tell ourselves, *"They must understand what this looks like. Surely, they know the hurt it's causing?"* or *"They really can't value us if they behave like this"* or *"He has never liked me. I knew from the moment he looked at me the first day, that I was never going to win".*

None of this is necessarily true. Because we live inside our own heads and our own thoughts are second nature to us, we may assume that other people think like we do and see the situation in the same way. The fact is, not only do other people behave in a whole range of different ways, they also think differently, hold different values and have different preferences for communication. They have different reactions to the same trigger. Just because someone does not behave in a way that meets our expectations, it does not automatically mean that they don't like or value us, that they are out to get us, or that they want to do us down.

We come into any relationship with our own filters, our own baggage from our life experience and our own preferences. Then we tell ourselves stories about the situation based on these filters. We extrapolate from behaviour to meaning and invest the story with emotion and messages to ourselves about what we must do.

Occasionally our stories may be true. And sometimes they're not! For instance, we may tell ourselves a story about fear – either our fear or someone's intention to instil fear, that goes like this: "*He has a reputation for ruthlessness: he's striding along: he's here to beat us*". (He may just be in a hurry.)

Another story might be about our need for control: "*I know how to do this, I've been doing this for ages and I get it right. No one else has this much experience and we must have the best result. I have to be the one to do it. I enjoy it: it's my task*". (It may be an explicit part of someone else's job description – and how will anyone else learn and get experience, if I always do it?)

In response to these stories, we react in habitual ways. With repetition, we entrench ourselves in these habits and escalate them. They became auto-responses which we have colluded with ourselves to create.

Remember the pattern that Controlling Parent and Rebellious Child can get into (referred to in Chapter 3). It might play out internally like this: "*He treats me like a minion. He'll use it against me. He only wants to aggrandise himself. Just wait! I'll show him*".

Notice the constant flow of stories you tell yourself, both about what's going on and about those around you. Stop occasionally: take out the current story in your head. Have a look at it. Is it true that:

- Because she rarely speaks to me, she thinks I'm hopeless?
- Because he has a private plane, he is greedy and selfish?
- Because they live in the centre of town they are loud clubbers?
- Because she keeps cats, she's a lonely recluse?
- Because we disagreed in a meeting last week, I can't speak to her in the café?

There's some flawed logic in here and a few assumptions that could do with being shaken out in the light of day. As you look at your stories, you may well end up laughing at yourself and having some fun explorations.

Stories like this are just some of the starting points which set us off unhelpfully in a conversation or relationship. And stories can be told from different perspectives, or helpfully rewritten.

The examples above are mostly stories that we tell ourselves about other people. We also tell ourselves stories about ourselves and undermine ourselves as we talk about our skills to our colleagues. Both types of story can make challenging times harder to manage.

Some people are likely to under-represent themselves when presenting how competent they are, and others are sometimes likely to over-represent themselves. It seems that in measuring themselves against a job description or person specification for a position, women are likely to apply only if they have 100% of the requirements, whereas men may apply with perhaps 60%.

This may tell us a variety of things about gender politics, self-fulfilling prophesies, the way we raise children and the way we describe and advertise jobs. It also tells us about how we may evaluate ourselves. You may like to look back to the section on limiting beliefs in the last chapter and check out how you, yourself, respond when you measure yourself against a list of role requirements.

When you under-represent yourself, underplay or deny your strengths, you are more likely to fall into a Victim role and to hook other people's negative responses. Moving from limiting perceptions of the world and our place in it, to perceptions which empower us, and help us present a strong face to the world, may involve reframing our stories and beliefs. When we reframe, we tell ourselves the story or belief in a different way, using words with different connotations, so that we alter our perception and gain a fresh perspective. As we alter our cognitive understanding of a situation, so we shift our emotional connection with the story. This in turn impacts on our levels of creativity, motivation and energy. To say nothing of our self-esteem.

Ira

Ira received his 360° feedback document. He read and reread it, carefully highlighting all the development points. He noticed phrases like *"your colleagues may see you as impatient to push ahead with results"*; *"some may see you as detached when there is a crisis"* *"you can be slow to recognise all the complex factors in the situation"*. Then he looked at the charts and graphs and noticed that not all the respondents had scored him above the *"good"* bar.

The story he then told himself was that his colleagues didn't like working with him, that he didn't take enough account of them, that he didn't cope well with crises or complexity. He was no good, was heading for a miserable performance review and that was the end of his career. Not only was his reading of the feedback very selective he had also extrapolated from the negative points to build a very negative understanding of his capacity and how others viewed him.

With the help of a coach, Ira looked again at the data; both the context of the comments on which he had previously focused and other aspects of the feedback. He noticed phrases like *"in a commercial environment, you are task focused and drive your team to achieve agreed outcomes within the timeframe"*; *"your exceptionally level-headed approach to problems supports calm solution-finding"*; *"While you often identify key issues in multi-faceted problems"*. He looked again at the charts and noticed that the respondent who consistently scored his performance lower than anyone else was himself.

His reframe went like this, *"I'm doing what the company wants me to do and I'm leading my team to achieve good results that meet deadlines. I'm really task focused and I can get the team behind me – however, I might need to keep an eye out for people who are finding the pace difficult and see what support they need"*.

"I stay really calm in a crisis and that helps everyone to find a good solution. Maybe sometimes it would be a help to other people to talk about how I deal with inner anxiety and clear my head when something tough and urgent comes up".

"I'm really perceptive about key issues and I don't always see everything. Actually, no one sees everything! Who sees things differently from me? Maybe there's a couple of people I can use as sounding boards when there's something complex going on, so that we pool our insights".

"Perhaps I'm actually doing OK. Even well in some areas. Now, how do I take the next step?"

Armed with this new perception, Ira moved from self-pity to being the hero in his own story.

Conflicts about expectations, roles and responsibilities

Conflict often arises from differing expectations about what we as individuals or teams are supposed to do and what other people or teams "ought" to be doing. We might get indignant because:

- No one has bought milk.
- No one has cleaned the office kitchen.
- Someone else sent out an email asking for views on something our team is responsible for.
- A peer gave a presentation that drew on our data without acknowledging our part in pulling it together.
- There is no money left in the budget because two teams have been working on the same project without either one knowing what the other is doing.

It may sound trite to say that sitting down to discuss expectations and what lies behind them is often the key to clarity and moving forward. Trite and yet true! Clarity about roles and responsibilities, setting boundaries to what we expect ourselves and others to achieve, supports harmonious team work. How to achieve that clarity is another matter!

Making diagrammatic baskets of our responsibilities and mapping how they fit together and complement each other can help us deal objectively with an area which may be fuddled if we simply try to hold it all in our minds. Drawing, sketching or mapping enables us to group ideas and deal with bigger, more complex clusters.

It seems, from recent research into neuroscience, that most of us can only work with limited numbers of ideas or concepts at any one time. We may be able to hold plus or minus seven things in our mind at any one time. Or the number of meaningful items or chunks of information which we can hold in our memory and usefully work with is far smaller. The key point is that there is a relatively low limit. After that it's helpful to group things into larger concepts. Think Monday, Tuesday, Wednesday, Thursday, Friday, Saturday, Sunday. It's quite useful not to have to run through each of these days individually all the time. The concept of a week gives us one idea to work with rather than seven and frees up thinking space to work with other concepts too.

Clarity of roles

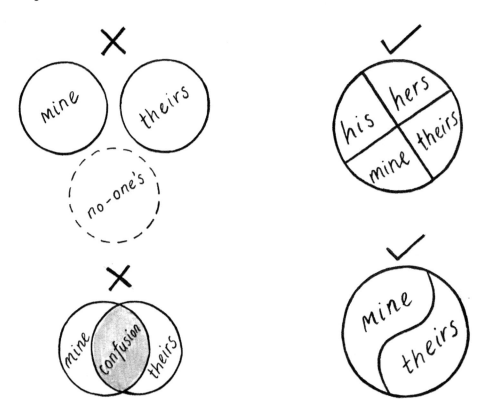

Try this

Working with a colleague or a partner, draw some circles or other shapes and write key words to represent different aspects of your roles inside each circle.

- Is one circle more densely populated than another?
- Do the same words occur in more than one circle/shape?
- Do you need to add more circles?
- What isn't represented in this diagram?
- Who else do you need to consult to get a full picture?

An alternative to writing straight onto a diagram, which might imply that responsibilities are fixed in a certain area from the start, is to write each responsibility on a separate post-it, to place all the post-its in a large undifferentiated group and then to allocate them to different people or teams. This approach allows for experimentation and rebalancing, and because the post-its are objects which can be physically moved, it's often possible to move them around with less emotion and more discussion.

Where the fuzziness about roles and responsibilities has been going on for a long time, you may need to have help from someone who is not embroiled in the situation and who will bring some impartiality. In a family, this could be a relative or friend, a trusted neighbour or a relationships counsellor. In a company, it could be someone from the Human Resources (HR) team, a senior manager, a union representative, or someone from a mediation service.

In both contexts, some of these people will have had training to help people work through differences in expectations and interpretations of other people's behaviour. Others will be benevolent connections who are well-intentioned amateurs with varying degrees of experience in working through disputes to mutually acceptable outcomes. There's a natural continuum and space for both kinds of support, though if things are getting tough, the earlier you seek help, the more likely clarity is to emerge without a prolonged struggle.

And it may be that we have to shift or reframe our attitudes or belief systems a bit before we feel comfortable enough to ask for help.

Holding the boundary

Some of the situations we've described above are about knowing what's in our remit and what belongs to someone else. People often have a strong internal concept of where the boundaries of acceptance, comfort and responsibility lie and may act on this concept even without having fully articulated it. It is evident in common speech in phrases like *"He crossed the line"*, *"She went too far"*, *"They were out of order"*. All these refer to the idea that we have boundaries of behaviour, power and personal rights which should not be infringed. These ideas are explored in assertiveness theory.

Assertiveness came to be popular in the last quarter of the twentieth century in places where people wanted to assert equality and challenge the coercions of privilege. It has flourished as an empowering behaviour and has simultaneously been treated with suspicion as a tool of social change. In general terms it is:

- A way to acknowledge and respect the rights of others and ourselves
- A system for engaging equally with people
- A method of keeping balance and cooperation
- An antidote to power plays

The assertiveness approach is based on the Transactional Analysis (TA) idea of keeping exchanges in the Adult to Adult domain in order to maintain factual balance and avoid undue and unhelpful emotional entanglement in conversations and activities. Assertiveness as a framework notes that in exchanges with others we tend to take one of three positions:

i.   Aggressive
ii. Assertive
iii. Submissive

There are echoes here of the Parent, Adult, Child framework of TA. The premise is about power. Where is the balance of power in the relationship or exchange? Who is taking power? Who may be disempowered?

We may hear a similar exchange play out in different ways, which each suggest where the balance of power lies.

Conversation 1: Greg and Pia

Greg: Do this report by close of play.

Pia: Absolutely. I'll start now.

The power is with Greg.

Conversation 2: Greg and Vlad

Greg: Please, would you do this report by close of play?

Vlad: No way. I'm busy. You'll have to wait till Monday.

The power is with Vlad.

Conversation 3: Greg and Indira

Greg: Please, would you do this report by close of play?

Indira: Right now, I'm in the middle of the skills audit for tomorrow. How can we fit the two round each other?

The power is shared.

Greg is the boss in all three situations. He is direct with Pia and he holds the power. He makes a polite request of Vlad, and he loses his power. Perhaps he is polite because he tells himself that Vlad is tricky and thinks he needs to tread cautiously. Yet it is not the way he asks that determines the reply. Both Pia and Vlad seem to respond in a habitual way based on some internal story: either *"You're the boss, I do what you say"* or *"Don't boss me around whoever you are"*. Indira, however, acknowledges that both she and Greg have rights and need open space to consider and balance them. That's the fundamental practice of assertiveness. *I assert my rights: I acknowledge yours.*

This recognition of equality of rights is also described as "I'm OK: You're OK" (a concept firmly rooted in TA). It illuminates our understanding of what it means to be assertive.

I'm OK + You're not OK = aggressive

You're OK + I'm not OK = passive

You're not OK + I'm not OK = despair, depression and doom!

I'm OK + You're OK = assertive (and calm and comfortable!)

When people want to improve their assertiveness, they are invited to consider and note what they believe their rights to be. For instance:

- *I have the right to say what I believe.*
- *I have the right to leisure time.*
- *I have the right to a safe working environment.*

We all sometimes feel that we (or others) are not getting the space and respect which we deserve, or that someone has crossed a line/gone too far. Then we need to reflect on what is going on; what rights we consciously or unconsciously think have been overstepped; and which of these rights we want to preserve. Then we need to find ways to maintain the boundaries.

Try this

1. Calmly ask the person not to do the thing that crosses your line. "*Please don't interrupt me when I am on a phone call*".
2. Or just ask them to do something that you perceive as missing. "*Please could you give me some specific feedback on my presentation before the end of the week?*"
3. And here is a formula for telling someone how you feel as a lead in to the request you are making:
   a. *When you …*
   b. *I feel …*
   c. *So, in future, please would you …*

Maintaining the boundaries

In the third example opposite, we give starters for three sentences, which together make an assertive approach. The ending of each is determined by the way it begins.

"*When you*" is followed by a specific behaviour e.g., *send the programme plan the day before the event*. It does not criticise who a person is, it just identifies a specific behaviour.

"*I feel …* " owns the emotion as my response i.e., this behaviour of yours has this effect on me. It might not have that effect on others. And this is how I respond. "*I feel rushed and as though I don't have enough time to plan, so I think less effectively*".

"*So, in future, please …* " asks for a specific behavioural change. We are not asking the person to change who they are, just to change a behaviour. "*So next time please would you let me have it at least three days in advance?*"

When we express what we need and ask for appropriate changes, it promotes a calm conversation which has the best chance of staying in an adult to adult relationship. We can do this when we understand where our boundaries are and are willing to communicate them clearly and to maintain them.

Sometimes we and others are tempted to resort to indirect approaches, which can be unclear, missed entirely, muddied by emotions or manipulative. Watch out for this.

Sometimes we may not notice that there is a power balance which is undermining our unarticulated boundaries. What about this exchange:

A: Someone left the hot tap left dripping again!
B: Oh, sorry!

A is obliquely accusatory while B seems apologetic and, perhaps, passive. The power seems to be with A though no specific accusation is made, and we don't know who left the tap dripping. If you have been B in exchanges like this, what did you feel? And have you ever been A and then later realised that you were the last person to use the tap? This exchange is an example of someone leaping in with blame before thoroughly understanding the situation. It's indicative of a blame culture, where the person doing the blaming assumes power and moral superiority. Quite the opposite of an Adult–Adult dialogue which allows exploration and learning from mistakes.

Numerous organisations say that they do not have blame cultures and that their practice is to encourage open conversations about mistakes and exploration of possible improvements. What we see on the ground does not always play out like that!

Some of the reason why we might default to blame may originate in the culture of our educational systems. Many subjects, skills and disciplines start from the premise that we find the "problem" and then propose a solution. That means first we blame … and then we tell! So, when we are looking for the problem we may be predisposed to blame others and, if our vocabulary reflects our training, we will probably use words like issue, problem, difficulty, fault and eradicate. Only later might we move to *solve*. When managers start with vocabulary like this, it is likely to be heard as a seek and destroy methodology.

People are likely to respond in one of two ways:

- Untrained managers may learn that this is the way we do things around here and so replicate the approach.
- People may complain about autocratic or fault-finding management to lots of others around the organisation … though probably not to the person doing the blaming. So, the manager becomes the problem! (see the Persecutor/ Victim roles in the Drama Triangle in Chapter 4!)

People now talk about learning organisations, meaning ones where there is a culture of learning from mistakes, of allowing exploration, of recognising difference and individual and collective potential for development. There is no place for blame. If you want to change your organisational culture, start by recognising what sort of obvious and oblique blame goes on and then work with people towards assertive conversations.

Holding yourself responsible

With rights come responsibilities. The right not to be harassed comes along with the responsibility not to harass others. The right to finish on time at the end of the day comes along with the responsibility to manage your time and your workload so that others can leave at the end of the day too.

We can hold ourselves accountable for remembering our responsibilities to others and for behaving in line with them. In order to do this, we generally need to do some work on what those responsibilities are.

Our colleagues may also want to hold us accountable for fulfilling these responsibilities. And of course, we can hold them accountable in our turn. Some of this process might be challenging.

If you want to be more aware of how you are showing up in relation to others at work, try this audit.

Try this

Draw up a three-columns table – Rights, Responsibilities, Behaviour

In the Rights column, think about all the rights you would like to have at work. Think about the organisation's values and add in any rights that connect with these values that are not yet on the table. Ask a few colleagues what rights they think they have/should have at work. Look at your organisation's policies to see if there are any rights enshrined in them. Now you may have quite a long list!

- Next, in the Responsibilities column, identify the implications of those rights in terms of your personal responsibilities.
- How do you need to behave so that others may enjoy their rights?
- Are the behaviours you are identifying good enough?
- Over perfect?
- How else might they be seen?
- What else might you do?

Discuss this with a colleague to get someone else's perspective.

The moment of truth then comes as you turn to the Behaviour column. Identify a few areas where tweaking your behaviour might make a real difference to others around you. Make some commitments about how you will behave in the future and write them down. Highlight them and hold yourself accountable for keeping to this commitment going forward.

Knowing how other people perceive our behaviour can help us keep to our commitments. Do they think we have changed? We need feedback! And we need to be able to receive it without being defensive. Sometimes our early family history or school experience has led us to be very sensitive to particular tones of voice or being asked to behave in a different way. We anticipate criticism and blame, go into a self-protective mode, focus on fight or flight and respond either aggressively or evasively. So, we don't easily take on board what we are being asked. It helps to plan and then practice a pattern of response to feedback so that we can hear, consider, absorb and learn from it.

Here's a seven-step process for doing just that!

Try this

1. The first step is to breathe!
2. Repeat back to the other person the criticism you think you have heard or the adjustment you are being asked to make, using an open and curious tone. *"So, you think that I have given too many tasks to Jana at once? And she's stressed out?"* This buys time and leads the other person to think they have been heard, so they get less anxious and are more likely to dialogue with you. It also helps to ensure that you have heard correctly and are not about to react based on a false assumption.
3. Thank them for the observation or the feedback.
4. Breathe again!
5. Check what they think would be a helpful adjustment.
6. Think about whether this is something you can incorporate (it may not be). If it is something you choose to change, talk about how you could do so, either to the person who's given you the feedback or to someone who can support you in adjusting your behaviour. Or both.
7. Make a note of what you intend to do and agree to check back in with the same person in a while to see whether they have noticed anything different.

Holding others responsible

Holding other people accountable for their commitments requires a different pattern. Some people find it straightforward to ask someone else to behave in a different way. Others find it difficult to do without turning into a commanding officer or a blamer. Yet others find it difficult to be clear because they worry about hurting someone else's feelings and so the message never gets across or is so smothered in euphemisms that they appear manipulative. This is not much use to anyone.

If we want to establish a learning culture, it's essential for everyone to get other people's observations on their behaviour and to have the opportunity to offer feedback as a developmental tool. Usable feedback is both clear and evidenced. Be careful! Most people fear that feedback is bound to be critical.

In Chapter 4 we mentioned that the ratio of praise to development points should be 5:1, finishing with a positive. Here's a way of scoring the feedback you give, evaluating how positive and how negative it is. This can give an idea of the impact it can have:

- An unconditional (global) negative, e.g., "*You're rubbish*", scores 0.
- An unconditional (global) positive, e.g., "*You're wonderful*", scores 1.
- A conditional (specific) negative, e.g., "*Each section in the process chart you presented should be clear individually so that people can see how their task fits*", scores 2.
- A conditional (specific) positive, e.g., "*You wrote an impressively succinct and focused executive summary in that report*", scores 8.

Use these types of feedback proportionately!

Aim to keep your scores high!

Feedback matrix

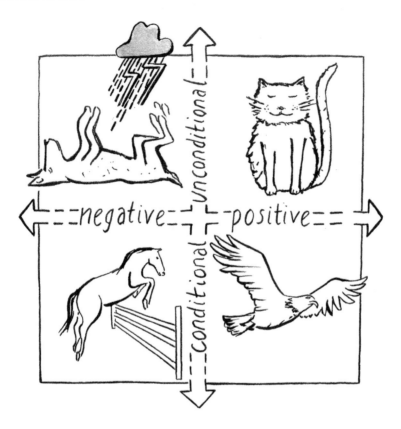

Too much unconditional praise feeds fat cats.

There is no recovery from an onslaught of unconditional negatives.

Conditional (specific) negatives encourage us to leap obstacles.

Conditional (specific) positives help us to soar.

Too much unconditional praise makes us complacent and stifles the space for growth.

If you find that you also need to ask someone to change their behaviour in line with their responsibilities or the organisation's policies, here's a different five-step process which might help you

Try this

1. Give a positive, evidence-based piece of feedback (a conditional positive as in the description above). *"Thank you for being in the office to help May when she arrived. She obviously found it easier to relax because you were there already and gave her a welcoming smile as she came in"*.
2. Say what you have noticed that is not up to the mark. *"And for the last few days, I've noticed you coming in at about 9.15"*.
3. Say what the policy is or the what the job requirements are. *"We've got a start time for everyone of 9.00"*.
4. Say how 2 does not match 3. *"When you arrive at 9.15 it's after the time that everyone is due to start and other people either resent it or start arriving later too"*.
5. Ask for the change you want to see. *"So please arrive on time in future"*.

Of course, you could make this into a four-step process, missing out step one. However, that first step may help you establish that you see positive aspects to the person's behaviour. It may also lead to their feeling positive, which may help them to be more open to what comes next. It must be evidence-based for it to be believable and for it not to be perceived as manipulation.

Difficult conversations

It's common to blame the other people involved for making particular conversations difficult. Labels that we often use to describe conflictual patterns include "power struggle", "bullying", "harassment" and "toxic relationships". All these labels carry a heavy emotional content, tap into our vulnerabilities and may trigger self-defeating stories about our powerlessness.

The shadow of imagined power

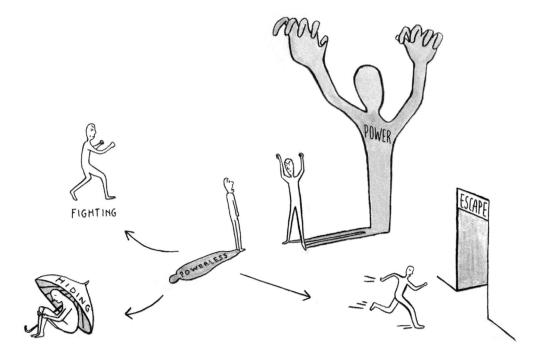

As we look at the person we blame for the situation, we might demonise them. The image of the other becomes hugely magnified. They grow in our minds to dominate the whole scene. We attribute more and more power to them and perceive ourselves as the innocent and powerless victims. We shrink in our self-esteem and self-confidence. Then our primitive defence mechanisms kick in: freeze, flight or fight. We find ways to hide, escape or take the aggressor on.

Some of these reactions might justifiably be to do with self-preservation and we do need to know when to run. Knowing when is key. If you like the occasional tune, you might look up a memorable song, "The Gambler" by Don Schlitz, which dispenses the wisdom of knowing when to hold your cards or when to fold them; when to walk away and when to run. What it does not include is when to call for support, which is also valuable in situations where you feel threatened.

Job–hopping or all–out war are not the only solutions to work place conflict, and not every situation escalates to the point where leaving is the only way to preserve our sanity.

Editing our stories about conflict

Some meetings and conversations are difficult because the subject matter is challenging. Some are difficult because we perceive that the people are difficult and uncomfortable feelings are triggered when we are with them. We see ourselves as being in conflict.

The pressures that cause this interpretation may originate primarily internally, or externally: from within ourselves, the rules by which we operate and the stories we tell ourselves; or from the expectations of people around us and the norms of the organisation or system which we work or live in. However, it takes two to tango. Despite the temptation to blame other people for what is going wrong, it is how the internal and the external interact that is the key to how we experience conflict and find our way through.

Many conflicts arise because of unquestioned assumptions, blind spots, lack of voice, unmet needs, fear or differing views about what is "right". Sometimes these are pressures linked to survival – for example where there are financial pressures – sometimes to questions of social acceptability and identity. Whatever we might think of the hierarchy of these differing types of need, they are all real and may come into play. How we react, and whether we react in a knee-jerk habitual way or with conscious choice, are key to our success in navigating stormy seas.

The first part of conscious choice is noticing which aspects of our interpretation are internal, our story about who the other person is. We can edit this story.

The next steps are adopting techniques to support the new story and to grow our strength. These include the assertive approaches earlier. You might also like to use a visualisation.

When we have magnified a person's power we can use a visualisation to minimise it. You might find one which can also amuse you. Here's a few that have worked for other people:

- Imagine the person as a camel.
- Imagine the person as a balloon, where suddenly the air is let out and it either spins off making rude noises or withers deflated to the floor.
- Imagine the person as a character in a TV drama – see them on the screen, drain them of colour, turn down the sound, turn them off.

If you want to explore this sort of technique further, look up some practical NLP, (Neuro-Linguistic Programming), tools.

Finally, find ways to take care of yourself! Reassert your strengths and note down appreciative comments that others make to you, to reinforce your self-belief in the face of hurtful behaviour. For instance, try the golden glow technique in Chapter 7.

Successful outcomes from difficult meetings

It's quite common to feel nervous about some kinds of meetings, so nervous that in some instances we would rather avoid them than go through with them. People tend to build up a picture of the things that might go wrong, anticipate opposition and tell themselves that they aren't any good at that sort of meeting. We know – we've been there!

Having a framework for what you are planning to say and rehearsing it in advance can help build your confidence. So too can controlling your breathing and visualising successful outcomes.

Visualising the outcome

If you focus on difficulty, you are more likely to find difficulty and not know how to respond. If you give yourself time to focus instead on the positive outcome you desire and bring your attention to your breathing as you do so, you will distract your mind from searching for a way out, relax and allow your unconscious mind to get into flow and access its own innate knowledge and inventiveness, leading to a better outcome.

Here's a visualisation process to add to your toolkit.

Try this

Before your meeting, find a quiet space to sit and prepare.

Imagine the person with whom you are going to talk, leaving the meeting at the end feeling satisfied with the outcome. Picture this person. How are they standing? What do they say as they leave? What does their face look like? Picture them smiling, standing tall, shaking your hand or making some positive gesture as they go.

Imagine yourself as this person leaves the meeting satisfied, standing tall, smiling, shaking hands. How do you feel? What's your face like? How are you sitting or standing?

Create a strong image of all of this. Breathe deeply and evenly as you allow it to become stronger and clearer.

Then in the meeting itself, hold this image in your mind from time to time. If you are at a loss for what to say, breathe and think of the positive image of the end of the meeting. Only then allow yourself to speak. If you are knocked off-balance by an unexpected response, breathe and pull up this image in your mind. You will find what you need to say.

Win-win technique

Sometimes we have to manage people who seem to want very different things and who are pulling against each other, not listening, not ceding any ground and in the end damaging the ability of the team to move forward. So, a win–win framework can be helpful in situations where there is divergence of opinions or conflict.

The process assumes that you have permission in some way to facilitate a discussion between two people who are at loggerheads. Although this may not be part of your official role, the principles behind this approach are very useful and can be borne in mind and modified if you are ever in contentious situations at work.

In this process, we presume that the people concerned each have a valid perspective, given where they are coming from, and that there is the possibility of finding some common ground.

We also presume that on the whole people prefer not to live in conflict and that finding a way forward without losing face is a relief. Even if we have a smidgen of doubt about the people we are talking to, following this process gives them the chance of achieving a positive outcome in a way that recognises and respects their concerns and points of view.

There is a presumption too of equal value. Each person gets equal time. Each person is listened to. Each person is assured of confidentiality (within the boundaries of the law and whatever binding policies there might be about disclosure of certain activities in your organisation). Information may of course be shared by agreement.

Try this

1. Clarify in your own mind the process that you are going to follow and why.

2. Talk to each person individually to explain how it will work and get their agreement to the outline of the process.

3. Spend time with person A, asking about their view on the situation; finding out the reasons behind their views/behaviour/feelings; exploring what their values are and what their stake in the issue is. Listen and check back that you have heard accurately by summarising key points or paraphrasing what you are hearing. Avoid commenting on what is being said.

4. Spend time with person B, going through the same steps as you have with person A.

5. Bring person A and person B together. Give each the opportunity to talk about their concerns and views without interruption. Ask person A to respond by acknowledging what they have heard of person B's point of view and explaining the impact for them *"I've heard that you were upset when you were asked to move desks because of your previous experience. At the time, I felt you were taking over my space"*. Encourage reciprocal responses so that each person gets a fair share of time. Draw on the "power shared" approach described in the earlier section on assertiveness.

6. Establish with them what the common ground could be.

7. Ask them to identify some options for action that could move them both towards achieving the common ground.

8. Facilitate a discussion of the options to identify what steps each will take next. These might include how they will communicate to other people about their discussions and their agreed actions. Establish how they will hold themselves and each other accountable for what they have agreed!

The listening without judgement is a vital part of the process. When people are listened to and they think their ideas have been heard, they are less likely to be defensive and more likely to be open to discussion and different points of view. Listening and saying "*I hear you*" does not cut the mustard. Reflecting back what you have heard and checking that you have got the key messages until the other person tells you that you've got it right, is an essential part of the process.

Negotiating

Meetings often include some form of negotiation. Some people find it particularly challenging when they need to negotiate to achieve a desired outcome – or to avoid a worst-case scenario. This could be a situation where you must represent your company and reach an agreed deal with a supplier or competitor. Each of you wants to get the best deal for your company. It could be a personal situation such as negotiating the purchase of a house. It could be negotiating a salary rise or professional development opportunity with your employer.

Sometimes we are held back by limiting beliefs of what we can achieve, so we are not ambitious. Sometimes we are held back by fear that we will be done down and lose out. Sometimes we just don't know how to go about the negotiation.

Negotiating – The hidden process

This is what often happens.

X, the seller, opens the bidding with an ideal scenario. The figure is likely to be a lot higher than he or she will settle for. In some cases, it may be half as much again, in others twice as high, in yet others ten times as much! The difference will depend on culture and style and is concealed from Y. X would be delighted and even amazed if Y met this price.

Y, the buyer, rejects X's suggested price and instead offers an ideally low price. This figure is likely to be a lot lower than he or she will settle for. In parallel to X, the differential between the ideal and the acceptable is concealed. Y would be delighted if X sold for this price.

In both their minds, there are both questions and secrets. Both have a band which would be acceptable. Both have a sticking point or deal breaker. If Y offers less than X's sticking point, the deal is broken. If X demands more than Y's sticking point, it's a case of *"On your bike"*.

In both their minds there are the questions:

- *Can we bridge the gap?*
- *Where do we meet?*

So, before the meeting, decide where your boundaries are.

- What would break the deal?
- What's your acceptable range?

Draw out a scale, mind map or diagram to show the boundaries of the ideal, satisfactory, acceptable and out of the question. You might allot colours to each section, especially if you do the mapping on post-its, which for some people would help the concepts to stay in their minds. For instance, green might be your ideal position; another colour – very satisfactory; another colour – what you would negotiate fiercely over, but still accept; red – what would make you walk away.

Make notes in advance about the levers, which might move the other party towards your desired outcome.

- What benefits might the other person get?
- What might *you* be prepared to give, if something else gave too?
- How far might you be prepared to go, if the gloves came off?

During the meeting, stay calm. It's a process, not a personal attack. Make notes. Keep your face neutral. Visualise where you are on your diagram or scale as the negotiation proceeds. If you plotted out your positions in colour, ask yourself where you are on the spectrum. What would move you away from the danger zone and towards the ideal?

Visualisation can help to relieve stress on your mind, so you hear more acutely and think more clearly. Hold the deal breaker close to your chest. If you reach it, walk away calmly. You decided beforehand the point beyond which you would not go, so that is that and there will be another way forward.

Many negotiations are not about money at all, so as you prepare, the ideal and the deal breaker will be expressed differently, in terms of time, activity, role, proximity, behaviour etc. Even when it's about money, of course, negotiation is not just about money. Other factors could influence the situation or make an almost unacceptable offer acceptable.

Other benefits might include recognition, support for a new project, advertising your product to a wider market, additional holidays. Decide before the meeting what you might offer and what you might accept, so you have these ideas up your sleeve if necessary.

Generally, a negotiation process goes stage by stage, sometimes with very little apparent shift in position by either of parties. Time is a hugely important factor. Just sticking to your point for a long time may wear the other down. On the other hand, if you know that time is very important for you and you have a shrewd suspicion of what will be acceptable to the other person, you may want to jump straight to your last acceptable offer, simply to save time and toing and froing. It's your call. Time and uncertainty both have costs, so enter these into your calculation and your prior thinking.

Knowing where your deal breaker is, at what point you will stick and when you will exit if you must, helps you to feel strong in the negotiation. When you feel strong, you look strong too, so the other person sees you as a more formidable negotiator. Visualising your sticking point as an iron fence or unbreachable barrier can help you feel strong.

If you lose the deal, which by the law of averages sometimes happens, it can be tough to deal with. There is an emotional impact when something is lost. Some moments of grief, even if these are brief. A frequent human reaction is to freeze (one of those F … reactions mentioned earlier). It's also normal to move on from the immediate shock, through a series of steps that leads eventually to acceptance. There is more on how to deal with the slough of despond and how to get a perspective on your response to unwelcome change in the next chapter.

Motivating yourself and others

The idea of benefits alongside the main offer, is a reminder that different people are motivated by different things. Some people like to work in a team. They would make a mistake if they assumed that everyone liked this and would find team working a reward. Others like to be involved in fast moving projects and change. They'd be wrong if they thought all the people who report to them liked this too. Some want recognition and overt praise, while others are more motivated by a project coming to fruition. Some are galvanised by an overall vision, others just like to know that they are doing their job in manageable steps that they can recognise.

Knowing what motivates yourself and others is useful in many situations: when you want to influence different members of the team, when the going is getting tough and you want to lift your own or other people's spirits, when you want ownership of a project, when you want to harness your colleagues' discretionary energy.

How might you know what makes your team feel good? The personality/ behavioural profiles which we wrote about in earlier chapters often suggest typical motivators for groups of people with similar preferences.

Staff surveys can be helpful, though if they are anonymised, you will find out about the range of motivators in the team and maybe the ones which the majority favour, rather than individual preferences.

How about asking people directly? The personal attention and listening that goes with a conversation about what makes someone feel rewarded and positive at work, is often a great motivator in itself.

And don't forget that praise is a huge encouragement to almost everyone – providing that it is specific, relevant, appropriate and personal.

Staying balanced in the face of harassment

Conflict may sometimes escalate to bullying or harassment. This is a specialist area where the following apply:

- It is hard to bring and win a case against someone we are calling a bully.
- Organisations have protocols for escalating any accusations of bullying, so the case may quickly get beyond your control.
- The person doing the bullying may have an unassailable power base.
- It's extremely hard to collect incontrovertible evidence.
- The "bully" may have infected the culture so that group culture perpetuates it.
- Colleagues may be fearful of potential consequences if they put their heads above the parapet and stand alongside you.
- Bringing the case to Industrial Tribunal, or other legal process, is likely to make some relationships more strained.

In the face of all this, how do you survive and what are your choices?

Here are some tips about how you might stay strong and balanced as an individual. They boil down to:

- Share.
- Be assertive.
- Visualise the positive.
- Stand in the other person's shoes.
- Remember your values.
- Discover common ground.
- Persevere.
- Affirm yourself.

Share. If you keep the hurt locked inside yourself, it's difficult to deal with and come out sanely on the other side. So, find a safe space and a reliable person and share!

- Sharing helps as a reality check – is what I think is happening, really happening?
- Sharing helps to bring hidden threats out into the open, where their power can be diminished.
- Sharing lets other people know what is going on, so they can support you.
- In some situations, sharing lays down evidence in case you or the organisation you work for need to take action.

Be assertive: Remember the assertiveness techniques we have described above and use them before the behaviour becomes an established pattern. This may include describing to the person concerned how you feel when they behave a certain way and asking them to change their behaviour. Make requests in line with company policies. Imagine yourself as steel within, powerful and strong.

Visualise the positive: Visualise positive outcomes to your meetings. Imagine how you will look back on this meeting from the future, knowing that it has contributed to your success. Imagine both you and the other people involved leaving the meeting smiling.

Stand in the other person's shoes. If you can, think that the other person has been formed by a particular set of influences and values and has learnt a way of behaviour from this experience. Seek to appreciate their perspective. Very often bullies have themselves been bullied. This does not excuse behaviour which hurts others. Understanding may, however, make the behaviour feel less personally directed.

Remember your values. Be clear about your own values and principles on which you decide how to act and be prepared to explain. Hold on to them like a guiding light.

Discover common ground. Find out, if possible, where the common ground lies. It may be small. Whatever it is, it is a potential starting point and foundation for more constructive working.

Persevere. Be prepared to persevere. Rome was not built in a day and it may be that your relationship will never flourish fully. However, drops of water eventually wear down even the hardest of stones and with persistent repetition, you will be able to establish your boundaries for what is acceptable behaviour, even if you have to enlist support from others to help maintain them.

Affirm yourself. Have a bank of mantras or positive affirmations to help you grow your courage when you are wondering whether you have the strength to say what you really want to say in a meeting. Here's a few to try:

- *"Feel the Fear and Do It Anyway"*
- *"False Evidence Appears Real"*
- *"Even a small step forward is still progress"*
- *"Choosing how to act makes me stronger"*
- *"I am powerful and strong"*

For reference, *Feel the Fear and Do It Anyway* is the title of a book by Susan Jeffers which offers techniques for affirming yourself, confronting challenges and choosing positive action. There are all sorts of examples of reframing your inner language to help you form positive beliefs and affirmations about what you can do, so you move into a more powerful place of choice.

"False Evidence Appears Real" is an acronym for FEAR and a reminder that we are sometimes held back by things we imagine or assume rather than by a realistic assessment of what might happen.

And repeating *"I am powerful and strong"* has an extraordinary effect on what we think we are capable of, how we hold our bodies and how others perceive us and therefore respond to us.

Chapter 6

Dancing in the moment

Dancing in the moment

The one thing we know for sure between birth and death is that things will change. Our life, work, relationships and the demands on us will change, and often the changes will be unpredictable and take us unawares. Economic and political circumstances are often volatile. Technology changes faster than we can envisage. Skills that were useful when we were young become outdated or redundant. Leaders are told that they need to be agile. And sometimes we could all do with a bit of help with our agility!

Let's focus more on living with uncertainty and longer-term sustainability. On keeping going and remaining true to ourselves in a changing and challenging environment. On functioning healthily in groups or organisations, where there are complex and varied dynamics and repeated change.

Of course, some people enjoy constant change and find it invigorating. Others, probably the majority of the population, would prefer time to adjust and are comforted by stability. If you are a fun loving flexer, your colleagues may want to slow you down. If you are a steady stepper, your colleagues may want to put a rocket under you. Either way, there is discomfort.

Responding to unwelcome change situations

If we are finding forthcoming or actual change uncomfortable, what might be getting in the way for us? It could be:

- Having a fixed view of how the world should operate
- Waning determination and enthusiasm
- Not believing that change is possible
- Feeling fear
- Disliking uncertainty
- Feeling overwhelmed by tasks; unable to reflect or plan how to navigate the change
- Not knowing how to keep going and giving up hope.

You will notice that the interferences we list here are all internal ones. The area over which we have most control! What good news!

From our own experience of resisting change ourselves and observing what happens around us, we know that these underlying internal interferences can lead to all sorts of behaviours which make the situation trickier to deal with.

So, for instance:

- *Raging against the change.* Blaming managers, colleagues, the economic situation – anyone and anything becomes a legitimate target for our contempt and anger.
- *Withdrawing co-operation.* Either actively or passively. Actively by openly refusing to comply or adapt. Maybe walking out. Passively by saying we agree, doing lip service to new requirements but either not fully carrying them out or undermining our compliance with contradictory statements or behaviours.
- *Fighting tooth and claw.* Pulling in the combined forces of unions, colleagues, networks, friends and family to defend the rights of our position and, if possible, defeat whatever change is in the offing.
- *Hiding our heads in the sand.* Hoping that if we ignore the change for long enough, it will go away, and we can emerge unscathed.

How well do these behaviours work in terms of either stopping change in its tracks or helping us to navigate it and thrive?

Hiding our heads in the sand: totally ineffective in stopping change. If our heads are in the sand, we're stuck where we are and have no influence on what's going on around us and we can't run from peril. We might as well roll over and die! And while the world may not look so threatening when we can't see it (because our heads are in the sand), when we pull them out and look around, we are likely to find the change even more difficult to deal with, because we haven't been able to gradually adjust, or we've simply been left far too far behind.

And by the way, it's a myth that ostriches bury their heads in the sand to avoid trouble. They are some of the fleetest of creatures and are far more likely to run. They also wield a hefty kick, capable of slaying many a predator. In extremis though, if nesting, they might lay their neck and head on the sand for a while to avoid being seen.

Fighting tooth and claw: may stop change, at some cost. People who fight as far as an industrial tribunal often end up leaving the organisation, because the damage to relationships has been so great. Cost/benefit is difficult to weigh up, though the fight may result in better conditions for others.

Taking the fight to the enemy's camp does tend to up the antagonism. Defence mechanisms come into force, positions become entrenched and the fight gets harder. It's rare to emerge from the battle unscathed mentally and often impossible to count the cost in advance.

Withdrawing cooperation: generally ineffective in stopping change in the long run and may result in loss of job along the way, especially if you do this in isolation rather than as a group. You are less likely to gain the credibility to influence change positively if you refuse to discuss it and negate every aspect. So, somewhat like the outcomes if you sticking your head in the sand, you may find that the eventual change leaves you behind or is harder to deal with when you do eventually re-engage.

Raging against change: most often ineffective. Raging may make it more difficult for the people you blame to implement change with the result that they lose trust in you, leave you out of decision making processes and withdraw their support for you in future situations. Raging against the wider context, economic trends and political failings, rarely stops change by itself.

Anger against both people and situations may make us feel better for a short while, but as a long-term strategy is destructive to both ourselves and others.

We get blinded by our feelings; react irrationally; repel others because the strength of our emotion is difficult to deal with; wear ourselves out.

Long-term anger stops us from being in a place of choice and is disempowering. Short-term anger may cleanse us but is most useful when it can be converted relatively soon to motivation for a mindful choice of response.

Choosing to react differently

Part of the message of Don Schlitz's song "The Gambler", cited in the previous chapter, is that every hand is both a winner and a loser: surviving rests on knowing what to throw away and knowing what to keep. And one way into knowing is through reading other people's faces; a skill that comes with experience and the ability to keep a steady head in a crisis. Reading messages from body language, mentioned also in Chapters 3 and 7, is a rich source of information.

So once again, back to internal control at the heart of how we experience and influence challenging situations. Back to knowing that it is our own choices which make the difference for us and often for others too. And we always have a choice. Just knowing that we do, is in itself empowering.

Creating hope for ourselves

Sometimes when things are difficult, it's as though we are at the bottom of a dark pit and we can't see how to get out. We may give up hope of an outcome and give up belief that we have any control in the situation. We may subconsciously wish that someone would magically appear, let down a rope and pull us out. Yet the answer probably lies in ourselves and the way we think about and picture the situation.

Lots of sticky situations start from a point of equilibrium and then get difficult. And common sense tells us, if we will only allow it to do so, that many of these can be resolved and we often have more control or influence than is apparent at first. Our own internal language and imaging are the keys to creating and sustaining hope and an upward trajectory.

Try this

Here's a few things to try to help yourself believe that there could be light at the end of the tunnel:

1. Draw a U shape with an arrow pointing upwards to the right. While things may get worse for a while, there will be positives in the outcome.

2. Draw a pit with a ladder leading out of it and yourself as a stick figure climbing up. Name one or two of the rungs of the ladder as actions you need to take.

3. Think of yourself as the animal you would like to be in this situation – if you were a panther, how would other people see you reacting?

4. Purge overgeneralisations and distortions. Instead of thinking, "*Nothing good will ever come out of this*", try some specific and positive reframing such as, "*We do want to achieve better outcomes. Working on it will help us to get there*".

5. Break the situation down into chunks. Identify what is in your control, what is within your influence and what you cannot impact on at all. Work on the first two of these areas.

6. Think yourself into a positive future and look back to now. As you imagine this positive destination, maybe a year down the line, look back at the path you have travelled to get there and think about a) what you would be pleased that you had done b) what you would regret not having done. Focus on these key things.

7. Look for the evidence and confront it. Remember that FEAR is an acronym for False Evidence Appears Real.

Understanding the change process

Sometimes when we are in the midst of change, we may think that we are alone in this uncomfortable process and be tempted to think of ourselves as victims. It might help to know that discomfort and a range of emotional reactions are common to most people's experience of change situations – and most people come out more or less all right in the end.

We are normal – and we can survive!

A very commonly used model to help us understand the sequence of emotions that are often experienced in change situations draws on the work of Elisabeth Kübler-Ross, on the stages that people go through as they deal with grief or news of an impending death.

There are typical staging posts, which people reach at their own pace, depending on their frame of mind and the degree of support or challenge that they receive on the way. With time we can move from resistance, which disables us, to acceptance, which frees us for action.

Understanding the commonality of our experience can not only help us to move on personally, but also help us to adjust to other people's pace as they too adjust to impending change. While we may be moving on in the process, others may be streets ahead of us in how well they are accepting and incorporating what is new; yet others may be slow adopters and need time and support on the journey.

Thinking carefully about our relative positions will help us to understand ourselves and adjust our expectations of other people so that we all have the chance of a smoother transition.

Charting the relative stages in a diagram can also help us to look at the process more objectively. It helps to untangle the feelings and because we can see that there are further stages in the continuum of change, it can give us hope of emerging successfully.

The change process

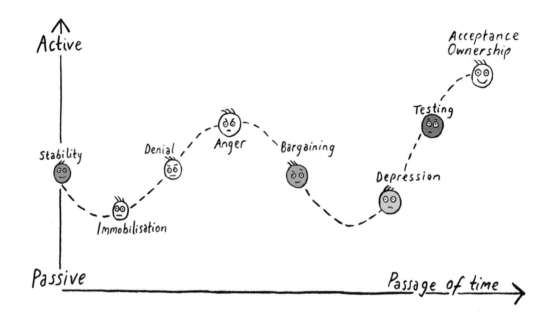

So, what are the stages we might expect to go through?

Before the change kicks in, we are in a state of relative stability. Often, when faced with demands that we don't like, we are tempted to idealise this state simply because we don't want to face the upheaval of doing something different. In reality, the status quo is rarely perfect.

Then we are immobilised by the oncoming change, rather like rabbits caught in car headlights. We don't know what to do or how to react. We then wake up but deny that this change could actually take place. When it doesn't look like going away, we get angry and set off on a path of fierce resistance, blaming other people or the context and trumpeting our determination to fight the change at all costs. If this has no effect, we bargain, hoping that if we offer favours, we will minimise the degree of change or secure for ourselves some favoured position. When this does not work, we sink into depression and once more become immobilised.

Fortunately, most of us rise again as phoenixes! Particularly if we are allowed to move through stages at a manageable pace and have appropriate support to move on. Then we can emerge to test the new reality and take steps towards accepting it and owning it.

Try this

- Using our change diagram as a model, draw a horizontal timeline for yourself from the introduction of the change to the future, with a vertical axis for the energy you experience in the situation.

- Make a mark on the vertical axis for where you were in terms of your energy when this change was introduced.

- Draw a line on this graph to show the stages of your journey through the change process, with a little face or symbol to represent the fact that it's your line.

- Draw other lines for the journey travelled by other members of your team or your colleagues.

- Think about what stages each of you might go through next and what sort of support you will all need to move on.

At different stages, people will benefit from different responses. If you are leading other people through change, it's helpful to remember that real life is not a straight line, but is full of hesitations, spurts and new starts. Keep your eyes on the end goal, watch out for the bumps and keep positive!

Responding to others in the change process

If people around you are full of fear, confusion and overwhelm and seem not to understand the thinking behind a proposal, accept their response. Encourage them to express their feelings, both negative and positive, and share them with others. Realising that they are not alone and that they are allowed to have an emotional response, can help them feel respected and lay the foundations for them to move forward.

If people are defensive and in denial, think amber light. Proceed with caution. Help them to look around and test out the evidence. How reliable is their information about what might happen?

When people are angry about the change and trying to regain control of the situation, recognise their feelings. Avoid getting into the personal and accusations about what "you" or "they" have done or might be about to do. Stay with it and watch for clues that they might be prepared to take some action. Be interested in how that action might make them and others feel.

When people move to bargaining and try to minimise the impact of the change on themselves and others, confront them a bit more strongly. Ask them about their purpose. Get them to check out the longer-term consequences for themselves and others of the solutions they are offering.

If people fall into frustration and depression, still find it difficult to cope with the change and keep focused on the loss, offer them support. Encourage them to identify what they can take responsibility for (what is within their control) and to take that responsibility.

When people begin to test out new alternatives, notice! Be positive. Tell them explicitly what is encouraging about what they are doing and help them to explore yet more realistic options for moving forward.

Above all, keep your mind on the fact that "we" will do this together. Involving others in setting the goal, defining the parameters and identifying the resources, will help you get there faster.

Try this

Set out on the journey with your team and keep everyone together with a set of questions like this:

- Where do we want to go?

- How will we know when we've got there?

- Where are we now?

- What could we do?

- Who needs to be consulted/involved?

- What's good already that we can build on?

- How do we feel about change?

- What are the cautions?

- What are the opportunities?

- What else could we do?

- What will serve the purpose best?

- What resources do we need?

- So, what will we do?

- When will we do it?

- Who will do it?

- When and how will we review our progress?

- When and how will we celebrate?

Keeping our focus in uncertain times

Given that the journey through change is often unpredictable and many people go through periods of self-doubt along the way, it's handy to have a few techniques to help us keep on track.

These are nearly always mental techniques – again something over which we can often acquire control!

First up is understanding that discomfort is a natural part of the learning process, so feeling discomfort may just be evidence that we are learning something new. The unconscious stages of our learning journey are far more comfortable than the conscious ones.

Unconscious incompetence (UI) is a state of blissful ignorance of what we don't yet know. *Unconscious competence (UC)* is a flow state, when we perform multiple tasks at the same time with consummate ease and grace. Sometimes we want to jump straight from the first of these to the second. Life just isn't like that!

The in-between stages, when we are all too aware of what we don't yet know or of the fact that we are performing appropriate actions but still need to think very hard about what we are doing, can be painful times of self-criticism and self-doubt. These are the *conscious incompetence (CI)* and *conscious competence (CC)* stages: in both we are very aware of our own performance and the amount of energy needed to keep focused on how we are doing what we're doing.

Worry not! These stages are part of the journey to mastery (though we are all a work in progress, rather than completed masterpieces, and there will always be some part of what we want to do that is in the discomforting middle section of the competence ladder).

One step too far

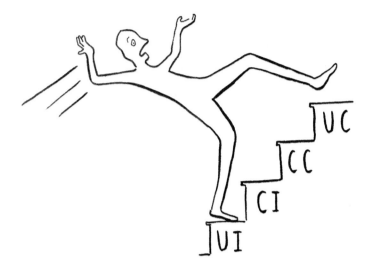

One step too far on the competence ladder!

If you overreach yourself, you will lose balance and undermine your ability to reach your destination …

Keep your eyes on where you are headed, the purpose for your changes and the positive outcomes you want. Keeping your mind on the "why?" will help you find the "how?" as you go. We can't know everything when we set out on the journey. Learning along the way is also vital.

Drawing on your inner strength

Quite apart from managing your own learning journey, if you are leading a team, you need to sound confident enough for others to follow you in times of discomfort. This may involve remembering the strength you have found in other situations and drawing on it as an inner resource. Your confidence as a climber may help you scale metaphorical mountains with your team. Your patience as a parent may help you surmount teenage tantrums in the office. Your inventiveness in the kitchen may help you think outside the box with a new work project.

Navigating change

Ruck

Ruck, a member of a senior management team, was tasked with leading some changes and engaging the team on the way. She didn't feel confident that others would follow her lead.

Then she remembered a time when she had acted strongly in a crisis. Her hobby was sailing. As captain of a yacht in a storm, her voice had deepened and strengthened, she had felt in command and sure of what she needed to do. The crew had done what she told them to do.

Rehearsing what she needed to say to the staff at work, she imagined herself as a captain again, with voice and stance to match. In doubt, she put out a hand to hold an imaginary tiller, keeping the yacht on track.

In challenging moments during the change process, she took a moment's breath, straightened her back, gestured towards her imaginary tiller and acted with the confidence of a seasoned captain, engendering further confidence in those around her.

Finding you own memory of when you have kept your eye on your destination and your purpose and others have followed, will help you keep focus in times of complexity and change. Remembering when you have led with confidence and commitment and then acting from that strong centre will, by a process of mood contagion, subconsciously influence others to accompany you on the journey.

VUCA – Our volatile, uncertain, complex and ambiguous world

It's the modern paradigm. We talk about leading and living in a VUCA world as though we need a whole set of new skills to deal with uncertainty and change. It's the very strong external and unpredictable forces of a VUCA environment, along with pace of change, that make it particularly challenging. It's the change that has always been there, writ large and speeded up. It's change on steroids!

For us, the sea is a fantastic image of VUCA – it's a constant state of change – uncertain, threatening, churning, surprising, influenced by strong forces. We need to learn to ride the waves because we know we can't calm them.

An insight into why it can be difficult to be confident in times of uncertainty comes from the work of David Rock. He draws on recent research showing that the brain reacts in a similar way to some types of social threat as it does to physical threats such as hunger and thirst. And some types of social experience trigger reward responses in a similar way to the satisfaction of physical needs. For both social and physical experiences, the same brain networks are activated.

The five crucial areas of social need proposed – status, certainty, autonomy, relatedness and fairness – are useful to us when we think about how people react to change situations. Are they motivated, or threatened? David Rock suggests that when these five needs are fulfilled, we are motivated. And when they are threatened, we have a reflex reaction of avoidance, undermining our ability to think clearly, problem solve, make good decisions, collaborate and manage stress.

When we relate this work to the rapidly changing environment of today, we get an insight into why many of us do not consistently operate at our best. Maybe a short period of change fires us up if we find new things exciting; however, prolonged change with no certainty undermines the ability of our brains to make patterns, predict, hypothesise and plan.

When we are struggling to respond resourcefully, simply understanding that we are not at fault, (when, as often, this is the case), can be a help. We could stand back and think that human evolution has been based on the ability to predict enough about the environment we live in to survive. When change removes that predictability, we may at some level fear for our survival, and react accordingly.

What are the implications?

Sarah

Sarah's role demanded a lot of both her and the team. Huge targets, pressure to achieve immediate change with long term lasting impact. Spin round and create magic, like the fairy on top of the Christmas tree.

She reacted by planning, hoping to control the immediate future and making it manageable. The plan helped her answer questions, as she thought the team expected of her. Sticking with the plan gave her certainty. However, circumstances changed (as they do) in unexpected ways, and when this happened, she sometimes reacted sharply. Her unconscious read *"threat"*!

Tension passed down the team. Someone was brave enough to tell her. Working with a coach helped to change her pattern of response, giving more trust to the team, who subsequently shone.

Learning we may take from this example is:

- Planning in small steps helps create certainty.
- We can choose to change what those steps are.
- Being flexible in the face of change supports wellbeing and survival.
- Checking new choices against our principles and values supports our confidence to flex.
- Working on personal awareness can help us give more trust to others.
- Being both calm and open when we don't know the answer yet helps others to trust us.

When we pretend we know, yet don't, we damage our credibility and engender distrust. When we share the fact that we are not omniscient, people recognise sincerity. When we add "yet" we evoke hope in an eventual solution. And when we are also calm, ripples of calmness spread to others.

When we share the process and the intention, the purpose of what we are doing, we provide people with an answer to, "Why are we doing this?" This gives longer term motivation and supports working together collaboratively on the, "How will we do this?" which helps to create certainty.

Making and communicating decisions

"Any decision is better than no decision" the saying goes. This suggests that in a rapidly changing context we must keep moving. And much of the complaint we hear in the organisations we work with, is about decisions: they are untimely, they are inconsistent, they are not communicated, the wrong people are involved, the right people are excluded.

It is not the brief here to deal with the organisational structure of strategic decision making. Rather, the focus is on how we each, at any level of an organisation, make decisions, and how we may choose to communicate them to others.

People often talk about gut decisions. Neuroscience now supports the idea that we have often apparently made a decision before the point when we believe that we are weighing up the evidence and coming to a considered and balanced outcome. It appears that we are more likely to decide from somewhere deep within us, using a whole set of long-held and personal preferences and biases. Our brain's main role is to keep us safe and this drive will have fed into most decisions.

Since everyone has different experiences, a different history and background, we'll always get a more balanced decision if we are able to involve a mix of people and take a diverse range of views into account. To do this we need to spend time listening to each other with a genuine will to understand. We may notice that many people use this approach naturally on their personal decisions, they chat to several friends or connections to hear different perspectives before settling on a decision.

People often seek the prior experience of others or to hear from people who have no bias, no interest in their choice, no skin in the game. Those close to us are always interested in the outcome and cannot turn off their own agenda however hard they try. Imagine a parent trying to be unbiased about, say, a decision their adolescent child is making about studying abroad, leaving school as early as possible or joining the army.

So, in work/business too we may seek unbiased views from a coach, mentor, adviser or consultant. Or we may, in getting a team together, ensure that we are all aware of the agendas of others in the group as we discuss pros and cons.

How is a decision made?

We could:

- Just decide instantly on gut feel and immediacy.
- Spend time assembling all the available information and researching.
- Try to look at the question from different internal perspectives.
- Ask other people to gather different external perspectives.
- Gather a group, share data and discuss pros and cons.
- Write a brief and seek expert advice.
- A mix of some of the above.

Major factors influencing the approach you choose are:

- What is the scope of your responsibility?
- Who are the other stakeholders? If any
- What's the time scale?
- What's the impact?

Though we may use similar brain functions and processes to buy new coffee cups and to take over another business, the impact and risks are very different.

The cross reference of risk assessments is fundamental here:

- How serious is the risk?
- How likely is it to happen?

Another set of questions which might help us reach a decision are the so-called "Cartesian Questions":

1. What will happen if I do?
2. What will happen if I don't?
3. What won't happen if I do?
4. What won't happen if I don't?

Another way is to think through the decision from the viewpoints of the Parent, Adult and Child:

- What does my experience tell me would be a good decision here? (Parent)
- What does my gut tell me about what I'd enjoy? (Child)
- Stepping back and taking these two views into account, what do I now decide? (Adult)

Sometimes the circumstances dictate the method; sometimes we go with our own thinking preferences. All the above methods are more attractive to some thinking styles than others and all have advantages and drawbacks.

Many work structures seek to mitigate the risks of inadequate decision making by instigating limits to delegation, official procedures, checks and balances. Examples include a restraining mechanism like, *"I can only approve a purchase up to £5,000"* and emergency plans and evacuation procedures. You don't want to be havering about a decision if the building is on fire.

We can't make effective decisions when we are very stressed. What we need are pre-rehearsed procedures in case of crisis, so we know that when that alarm sounds we drop automatically into a pre-planned set of actions.

Things to think about as you consider your own decision-making skills are:

- How have you made your best decisions so far?
- What do you know about your learning preferences? Do you like to reflect carefully before coming to a decision? Would you rather think and act fast?
- What are the disadvantages of your preferences?
- How might you balance those out?
- What can you put in place as standard, before the point where a decision is needed, which will act as a support in the moment?
- Who or what is your best support in this?

When is a decision made?

Some of us like to think aloud and play with possibilities as we speak, forming plans by imagining a route, seeing a problem, backing up and restarting. This thinking aloud and changing as we go can be very disturbing to those who prefer thinking it all through before coming to a decision and then voicing that as a fait accompli.

This *"here is the decision: I've done all the thinking: no further discussion"* approach is similarly unsettling to someone who likes to hear the whole circuitous route to the outcome.

Therefore, when you are making and communicating a decision, which affects others, consider the recipients. What are their communication preferences?

In change situations, we need to be particularly sensitive, not just to personal preferences but also to differing individual contexts and different degrees of potential impact on different people. We must be entirely sincere ourselves and, at the same time, open to understanding other people's responses, not assuming how they will react.

When is a decision communicated?

In many circumstances no news is dangerous. We are social beings. And organisations have strong social structures and cultures which are not necessarily connected with the avowed business aims of an organisation. So, when change is in the air (note how we talk about unknown forces at work), or it is clear that a decision is being considered, in the absence of actual information, rumours and fantasies begin to emerge and grow. Better to give clear information even about the lack of information or the process you are using to gain it, than to leave fertile minds to make up stories, and share, and elaborate them. These can take a lot of time and energy to unpick and do a lot of damage before they are banished.

Staying with the decision

Shilly-shallying; deciding, then questioning immediately if we're right; veering from one decision to the next; all create uncertainty for us and for those around us. Of course, there are occasions when it's better to review a decision in the light of new knowledge, and it often takes the pressure off us if we know that we may choose to change our minds further down the line. However, overall, it gives both us and others more peace of mind if we can close the menu once the decision is made.

The image of closing the menu might be helpful. Having chosen chicken and rice, get on and order it! Don't start wondering whether instead your friend's choice of aubergine tagine is what you ought to be choosing too. Close the menu, put it down and enjoy the company and the meal!

Dealing with the consequences of change and tough decisions

If you take a bold decision and tell everyone what you are doing – expect flack. In the past, it might have been a crowd throwing rotten tomatoes. Now it's more likely to arrive by email or twitter.

Often in emails, everyone copies everyone else in, encouraging more and more extreme opinions, which correspondents expect others to endorse. A barrel of rotten tomatoes is finite. An email storm is not. Feeling gets whipped up and negative opinions and professional judgements may move from the cognitive and reasoned – "*it isn't the right time to make this step*" – to the affective, with emotional accusations of failings of a global and personalised nature – "*you're a big-headed idiot to do this*".

The temptation is to jump right in there, refuting accusations and getting increasingly caught up in the whirlwind, which is both time consuming and emotionally draining. Wait. To enter in the fray too early in a group response might be appropriate if it is a matter of sharing an organisation wide policy.

Otherwise you run the risk of entering into a ping pong of self-justification and blame which will only add fuel to the fire.

Keep clean. You are finding out what's in the air. Be patient, even though it may be hard. If possible, seek a rational input from a senior respected figure, pointing out where decision making responsibility lies, that everyone has different perspectives and that since many have been aired it's time to step back; that there may be other mechanisms for carrying forward the discussion more constructively if possible. Look outside this group if you need emotional support or a sanity check.

Wait again.

When you think the storm has spent its worst, or even calmed down, consider which correspondents to reply to on an individual basis. Thank them for the perspectives they have shared and their commitment to the cause, which may be the company's values, commercial intent, good of the department, or moving out of an impasse. Your thanks must be genuine. Make some short general points and a unique response which connects to a key aspect mentioned in that individual's email. Refer if possible to something you value in working with that person. You then have a starting point for a more constructive individual dialogue, maybe initially by email, then in conversation, which is a much subtler tool, and meaning can be explored and discussed.

Do not think you can get everyone completely on your side 100% of the time.

Gradually the group hysteria will die away; individual constructive relationships will emerge and you will learn and understand new perspectives which have the potential to help you avoid pitfalls in the future and lead more effectively. Gradually the mass of opinion will shift.

You may need to deal with outliers separately and with different support structures, but that's another matter. There are many who might support you including Human Resources professionals.

Individuals are more likely to offer help when they can do so on a 1:1 basis rather than sticking their heads above the parapet in a public situation. Individual criticism in a private space is easier to both absorb and respond to as there is less at stake.

Khalif

Khalif was managing director of a regional subsidiary of a nation-wide company. Recently promoted, he had been brewing ideas about how to make his unit more efficient and a better place to work. Over the years he'd had run-ins with the head of marketing, Trish, who'd been in the company since it was founded and had very fixed ideas about what needed doing and how it should be done. She had undermined his proposals for change on more than one occasion. Partly because she let everyone know how well she was doing, she had built up quite a power base in the company. With a couple of years to go to retirement, she wanted to go in a blaze of glory.

Khalif took HR advice about options open to him. He proposed a restructure, which would mean slimming down the executive team, as a result of which Trish might lose status. While this was still in the consultation stage, Trish sent an email to the CEO of the company, copying in all the managing directors of the other regional subsidiaries, the executive team and heads of department in Khalif's subsidiary, saying that her role in the company, which was so essential, was likely to be deleted.

One by one, people piled in to say how important it was to have a head of marketing in every subsidiary, how much they needed Trish and how unthinkable it was that she should go. From reasoned arguments about the role of marketing in commercial success, the emails got more emotional, suggesting that Khalif was new, out of his depth and arrogant; that he was undermining equality of opportunity and needed to withdraw his proposals.

Khalif knew that if Trish retained her position of influence for the next two years, he would be unable to make the changes he hoped for. He realised that this was not a decision that he could implement on his own, because of the danger of splitting and potential accusations of victimisation. He took a step back and asked the CEO, Mark, for his perspective.

Mark emailed the other directors of the subsidiaries to say that he had confidence in Khalif and that while they might wonder about how the proposed restructure might set a precedent elsewhere, it was Khalif's responsibility to sort out his own stable. Gradually steam died down. Khalif replied to emails individually, leading to 1:1 conversations, some quite robust, which laid the ground for building understanding and shifting the balance of opinion. While the work was not yet done, it was easier to move the team to change.

The strategy outlined before this story does not mean that it's easy to face criticism or that you will suddenly find yourself enjoying a fiercely critical group response. It is forged from experience, so you know you are not the only human being who has faced an onslaught. It offers a way forward, step by step. Many people find that this sort of pathway gives hope and builds resilience.

Mapping and managing influence

In the situation above, it is very likely that Trish had worked to influence people … and that is what led people to "pile in" supporting her. She may have done this incrementally over the years by building relationships, for instance by paying into a whole range of emotional bank accounts (see Chapter 3) or she may have rallied people at the point she was feeling threatened using a range of approaches and techniques to bring them onside.

We know both that we have to manage our own responses and that others are different from us with their own preferences and patterns. It is naïve to imagine that because we think something is the right way to go or thing to do, others will just naturally follow us. So, it makes sense when preparing for an important conversation, negotiation, meeting or deal to survey the field and see what we can do in advance to bring people with us. And to bring the people who will bring most others. Hence stakeholder mapping.

Earlier chapters described matching your style of communication to suit the preferences of the person or group. It is also important to make sure you are presenting to the right person in the first place!

In any situation we want to influence, there are a number of players, who are either more or less in agreement with us and our aims, and who are more or less influential. Our influence diagram opposite gives us a framework for mapping the impact different people may have on a situation. It allows us to look at how "onside" someone is. That means, how likely they are to support your view or espouse your cause. This is the horizontal axis. The other axis, the vertical one, is about how influential they are.

Someone may be hugely on your side but if they have no influence at all they are not very important to your outcome (other than as one vote … if it comes to that). So, mapping the potential players in a decision-making process appropriately on the model begins to show us where we can best employ our limited energy (and other resources) for maximum impact.

If someone has huge influence, we may want to start with them, as they would bring many others with them. However, if they are adamantly against what we are trying to achieve, we could spend a huge amount of effort for very little return. Imagine trying to convince the marketing director of a petroleum company to vote to double the tax on petrol and give it as a subsidy to windfarms!

Map of influence

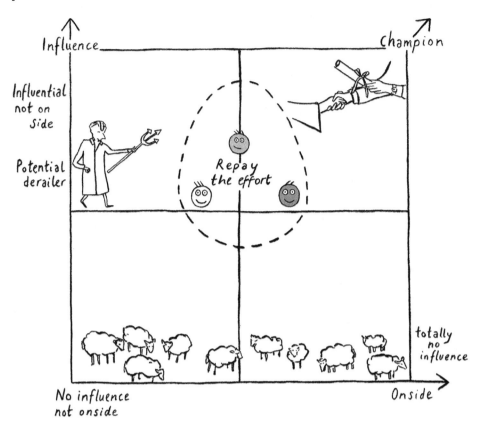

Try this

Take a blank version of the matrix and place post-its or objects to represent the stakeholders in appropriate places.

Keep asking yourself "Who else is important?", as we sometimes forget important people for a range of reasons.

Then look at the area near the top and around the middle line (marked in our diagram as "Repay the effort").

Decide where to put your energy for maximum pay back.

The people who have lots of influence and are only just offside are a
good investment of your time: it may not take very long to convince them,
and they will bring others along if you can get them to stand up in your
favour.

Spending a while mapping the potential contributors allows us to manage our
own time and impact to best advantage. And if we have done the
groundwork over time by building relationship, communicating well and
respecting people's otherness, then we'll have a much easier time explaining
and influencing. Many of us spend time building our case and rehearsing our
arguments, then use them in ineffective places and become frustrated with lack
of support.

Sometimes people will place us on their map of influence too! Who do you think
would like to influence you to their cause? And how do you react if you think
you are in the target group of maximum payback? It's worth exploring what your
habitual response is to people trying to convince you of a case. Do you go with
the person or the proposition? Would you agree to something for a friend which
you wouldn't consider for a distant colleague? Do you always need data or are you
more interested in eloquent presentation?

As you consider your own patterns, think about when it might actually be
useful to get a very different perspective on something. Often, we dismiss whole
categories of things because we decided long ago that they did not work for us.
Now might be the time to be more open to another viewpoint and to re-evaluate.
After all we'd like others to be willing to do that for us.

If you were to place yourself on someone else's stakeholder map, where your
impulse is to be on the offside position, what puts you there? Is that what you
really believe? If so, do you still really believe it? Sometimes things move on, and
it is appropriate to reconsider and re-evaluate. Allowing ourselves to check that

we still really believe in the positions we espouse, is good for us, good for our credibility and good for our colleagues and collaborators.

Mapping the people who might help us to achieve our dreams, and then mapping how we think other people might see us in their map, can be a way in to greater understanding of the value we bring to each other. What gifts have we got for the other? What needs might we be able to meet for others? If we do that, what might we like in return? How could we find out about other people's perspectives? Take time to reflect, ask, listen and reflect again as you plan your strategy for greater effect.

Mapping influence with objects

Making a map allows us to stand away from the issue we are considering and literally see it differently. If we make the map with objects, we can move them around, enabling us to rearrange things as we would like, check that things are as we see them and explore how we would like them to be. You'll find this sort of technique named variously as constellations, tactile imagoes, magic boxes and probably in other ways as well. It can help us to explore and unpick situations, teams, relationships, groups and patterns – indeed, almost anything which is made up of several aspects.

Objects can represent people or departments or tasks or parts of a role. They can also represent more intangible aspects, such as pressures and expectations. You may notice that people do this sort of thing naturally: sitting at a meal table someone may place a fork and say, "*So this is the CEO*", then a salt pot, "*and this is the Board*", then a plate, "*and this is the marketing department*" and so on. When this happens, we can invite the map-maker to continue by asking "*What else is there?*", "*Who else is important?*" until they seem to have completed the map (for now).

The next stage is for each of us just to observe it. It helps to have a neutral observer. If we are emotionally close to something, we see more when we externalise it with a sketch or a map, and even more if someone else is there to make neutral observations such as *"that one is further away than the others"* or *"there seem to be three clusters here"* or *"this is lower than all the other pieces"*.

These observations are facts about the map rather than value judgements, and they allow us just to see something literally. Sometimes that is a revelation. For instance, it can be amazing to notice that though a group are actually all equal, we have instinctively placed one piece further out while all the others cluster.

Try this mapping technique just as an example for yourself with a group or team you are in. In this first try you are not seeking to change anything, to improve communications or to influence. You are merely noticing what you notice! It makes a difference to see and move players rather than just thinking about them. Experiment during a time of status quo, so that it is a tool in tool kit when you really want to explore and find new approaches.

Systemic influences

Much of our focus so far has been on working with individuals. A few individuals together make a group, of course, and several groups make a system. The way groups operate creates organisational culture, which often exerts influence on others to behave in a similar way in order to fit. Sometimes this influence is pervasive and at the same time difficult to resist, because no one articulates the rules. Not to behave in line leads to the risk of social or professional isolation. To behave in line may subtly force us to act out of true to ourself. Everyone behaving in line may lead to narrowness of view and collective blind spots.

Mapping with objects as described above can help us to get a fresh perspective on what is going on in both systemic and psychological terms. Then we have a richer understanding to inform a decision about what we might want to do.

Try this

Clear a space on a desk or table. Choose an object to represent yourself. Place this in the centre of the space.

Think about the pressures that you experience. Maybe to work till the small hours of the morning. Maybe to go out drinking with colleagues at the end of the week. Maybe to cover up errors by blaming technology. Represent each pressure either with an object like a pen, or by arrow-shaped post-its on which you can write. Perhaps your choice of object or the way you write can represent how powerful these pressures are.

Place these pressures around you, closer or further away, clustered or separate, to represent how you experience them.

Where are they coming from? Find objects to represent individuals and groups that the pressures are coming from.

Who else is impacted? More objects or post-its.

Now look at the map you have created. What do you notice?

Where is most pressure coming from? Is everyone impacted in the same way?

Move to the opposite side of the map. What does it look like from here? What do you notice? And what if you look at it from another angle?

What could you be in control of here? What might you influence? What might you influence if you worked with other people? What might you be able to influence with time? What position would you need to reach in order to have that influence? And what is outside both your control and your influence?

The degree to which you can influence culture may determine whether you stick in a job and play the long game, or whether you create a fast-track exit-strategy! Whether to hold your cards or fold them. Whether to walk away or run. And mapping can give you the insight you need to make that decision.

Sharing, flexing and fun

There are so many ways of working with different perspectives and so many routes we can take as we learn to be flexible in our approaches, acknowledging our own range and the preferences of others and we've called it dancing in the moment. Sometimes we can literally dance … or do something similar. Movement, novelty, the unexpected, can lift the spirits, increase energy and help us move forward.

Many organisations encourage a range of movement options: hot desking, standing desks, exercise groups and classes, themed days. This is not new as a way of keeping people healthy, interested and committed. Years ago, every colliery and factory had its football team or band. Coincidentally Jenny's parents met when her father's London warehouse cricket team played the rural supplier factory where her mother lived! They both remained quite loyal to that company!

When did you last do something unexpected or fun at work? What might you try in order to hearten yourself and colleagues? To show people you appreciate them? To celebrate an achievement?

Our favourite example is a marketing director who, to celebrate a sterling achievement, suddenly burst up to one person's desk with a couple of colleagues all blowing jazzy party blowers and shouting and clapping! They threw streamers across the desk, hung a balloon over it and shouted a message of congratulation. They swirled into the room, celebrated and were gone in seconds, leaving chocolate and laughter behind them. They called it "flash mob endorsement".

This flash mob was briefly planned and appeared spontaneous. And these two facets of fun are interesting for the instigator. The fun, celebratory events and activities, which organisations plan, rapidly become part of the structure and so can cease to give the results intended. The first year we run a post-audit party it's new, a surprise and a treat; the next year it has to be slightly better, and if we don't do it in the third year, people are disappointed, and it affronts their sense of fairness.

Gifts and events for staff are so part of the fabric of people's expectations of their employer that there is even a tax-free allowance for them in the UK. It doesn't get more regulated than that! So, consider how to manage this potential escalation of cost and creativity.

If we have an endless supply of safe, varied, professional and ethical spontaneity that's ideal! And possibly few of us do. When we're operating in Creative Child mode spontaneity can tip into impetuosity. The consequences of that are often in the press and the courts. We need to balance light-heartedness and professional credibility.

Coincidentally, as we write this, on a train, we overhear two young professional women, who are travelling to what seems to be an important company event, agreeing that they are nervous about what to say to senior people at the formal dinner but that "*it'll be OK when we've got a few bevvies in!*" Possibly not the best plan for maintaining career progression!

Fun and social events are great at building team spirit and motivation. And some (appropriately) spontaneous acts become the stuff of myth and source of stories in organisations. These retold stories become part of how organisations understand themselves and express their value and culture.

Steve

Steve, a senior executive, was chairing a small meeting. He shifted in his seat to get more comfortable, missed the seat and landed in a sitting position on the floor. Because he was very tall, his head was just visible over the table top. Without missing a beat (he knew himself that he was not hurt), he continued to lead the conversation, straight faced and thoughtful. This became a significant story about his unflappability, work focus and deadpan humour and was much laughed over after the event. It was retold and retold, reinforcing company culture.

Bim

Just before Christmas, as numerous activities were in full flow in a college, a spot inspection was announced. As the inspectors descended the next day, tension was at boiling point. The duty manager, Bim, was on walkabout, and passing the theatre, went onto the dance floor. Kicking off her killer heels, she joined the costumed cast in the warm-up, wearing a business suit and with a brick-sized control radio clipped to her belt. People remembered for years. Her impromptu action calmed the anxieties of those around her and reinforced the values of the college: the students come first, what they do is valuable; we have nothing to hide. It became the stuff of legend.

These stories show us how culture is made in an organisation. When we choose to do something out of the ordinary, if it comes from authenticity and our values, it supports certainty, honesty, fairness and relatedness.

Chapter 7

Forging ahead

Forging ahead

Much of this book has focused so far on three main ideas:

- Building a greater understanding of the self
- Using our minds differently to shift the way we perceive and experience others
- Developing techniques to improve our interactions with others

Adopting new patterns is a first step. For long-term lasting impact we also need to add in self-care. This includes both awareness of what's going on in our bodies and effective use of time.

The body tells the story

The body and the mind are one system. As we respond to people, discussing, explaining, analysing, negotiating and doing all the work we might call thinking or mind work, our bodies constantly send us messages and signals.

Our minds affect our bodies. An extreme example of how some people are affected is burnout. Our minds have been overloaded and maybe we have been working very long hours. The body systems shut down to tell us to stop. However, we all respond in our bodies long before that crisis point, even if we ignore the signals we are receiving.

If we see a person we find threatening or enter a meeting we find challenging, we will probably experience physical symptoms: our heart rate may increase, our palms sweat, our mouths go dry. These and a whole range of other bodily responses happen constantly in response to our thoughts, perceptions and interpretation of our changing environment.

Our bodies also express long-established patterns of our experience and expectations of the world: we see these reflected in people's posture, gait, instinctive movements and physical responses as well as in the lines on their faces, the history of their illnesses, their skin tone and habitual gestures. It is striking how early this happens. Watch children. Do they smile confidently? Do they flinch or shrink? Are their shoulders back and their glance level? What are the patterns they are laying down at an early age which will become absorbed into what they think of as their personality when they are adults?

And because the body is responding constantly as we work and interact, it's important to notice this and take care of it. The simplest form of self-care in the moment is to pause. When in doubt, breathe. Several benefits come from this:

- Breathing gives the brain oxygen, so we have a better chance of thinking clearly.
- Breathing calms us because for a moment our attention is not on the threat but on the rhythm of breathing.
- Breathing creates a pause in which we and others have time to reflect and may become clearer and more resourceful. Both we and they have some space to self-manage.

We hear lots of health advice about balance: exercise, diet, relaxation, not overworking other people, not fostering a culture of presentism or neglect of a duty of care. If we overwork ourselves or continually place ourselves under excessive stress and just stick these types of self-care on top, we are unlikely to thrive. And if we do not thrive, others around us are unlikely to do so either. If we lose our own capacity, we are not much use to the team.

We have to develop accountability for ourselves and for what we model to others. It is our own duty to know how we are in ourselves and to support our own wellbeing. Not only will other people follow the example of what they see us do; we will also thrive. Practising mind–body awareness and self-care is therefore the foundation of great work and of great working relationships, not the medicine to take when things are going wrong.

Self-care audit

What self-care do you need to ensure you are at your best as you work and as you work with others?

If our body (our self) was the most important machine for the business to continue to run, would we run it without oil or till it overheated, would we neglect to give it fuel or clean the parts: would we just run it into the ground, urging it on with more force if it faltered? Or, if it was that most important machine, would we have a schedule of maintenance, which included review of how it was running and a budget to support necessary improvements?

Noticing how our body is responding and analysing the source of this response can help us to be aware of what we need to change – a working habit, a relationship, a way of thinking.

Some bodily responses are directly linked to the activity we are carrying out at the moment. Often, however, we carry a response from one interaction or event into another. I have a phone call which annoys me, someone comes to my desk and I snap at them. The snapping belongs to the phone call not the person. When this happens, the people around us jump to conclusions about our judgement of them, which may not be what we would choose if we were aware of where the bodily response was coming from.

When we react with irritation, people learn not to ask us for things because they fear that they are the source of the irritation. It may have a completely different source.

When we notice our bodily or emotional responses (and the two are almost inextricably linked), ask, "*Where does this come from?*" Then check to avoid leakage from one event or person to another, and work on eliminating or minimising the key trigger.

Try this

1. Take a moment at various points in the day to ask *"What is going on in my body right now?"*

    Interesting answers may emerge: e.g.,

    - My stomach is rumbling.
    - I'm clenching my teeth.
    - My shoulder is raised.
    - I'm slumping.
    - My hand/arm/back aches.
    - I'm frowning.
    - My heart is racing.
    - I'm tapping my foot.

2. Check what this is a response to. Ask *"Where did this come from?"*
3. Ask *"Is this what I choose?"*
4. Work out what adjustments to your body, mind, language, behaviour, habits, etc. you want to make.

Remember Mike who drummed his fingers when thinking about an issue? Others interpreted that as irritation. He probably didn't know he was drumming and certainly didn't know how this was interpreted by those around him. The body scan above would have brought this into awareness and given him more choices.

Caring for the mind

Self-care in the physical sense also includes resting the mind!

Time is often perceived as the enemy and the destroyer of peace of mind. People often complain that there is not enough time to do everything. As the world moves faster and we expect to travel from place to place more often, simply because it's physically possible to do so, we experience demands to fit more and more into the day. Yet we all face the fact that there are the same number of hours today as there were yesterday and will be tomorrow. A round twenty-four. Maybe, we think, a new technology will come to our aid and make jobs magically easier. Which brings us with circularity back to the starting point of our book.

We can't manage time. We can manage our own attention.

When tasks get out of control, it helps to have a system to sift what to do and a set of principles to measure competing priorities. The *Do-It-Disc* will help. It's a model which we, that is, Sarah and Jenny, developed some time ago as a way of sorting priorities, dealing with pressing matters that other people thrust our way and reminding ourselves of the need to stop doing and refresh ourselves. This updated version is the result of our work with busy leaders and of our reflection on our own ability to manage time and attention.

There are four segments of the Disc, of uneven proportions. Aim to spend the majority of your time on the right-hand side of the Disc, in the *Important and Influential* and *Rest, Restore and Review* segments. Keep expanding the proportion of time you spend there and shrinking the time you spend on the Urgent side of the Disc, much of which is generated by other people's priorities rather than your own.

Important and Influential: These are strategic tasks with the potential to give you direction, enable clarity and reduce crises. They include setting long-term goals, determining objectives and measures of success, building relationships with the team, planning how to use your resources, developing policies and procedures, planning how you will use your time and developing yourself professionally. When you spend your time on these tasks, you will reduce the time you need to spend on others.

The Do-It-Disc

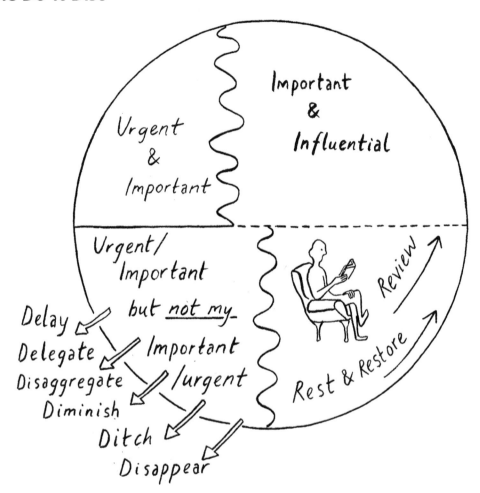

Some of these Important and Influential activities may not appear pressing or enticing at the moment. They may not hold the attraction of the new and may be less visible, adrenalin drenched and heroic than firefighting. However, if there is a fire in the building, time spent planning evacuation procedures will have been time well spent. People will leave the building calmly and lives will be saved.

Plan when to do your important and influential tasks and do them when you have planned to do them.

Urgent and Important: There will always be crises. Accidents. People going off sick. Theft. Fires. Dealing with crises raises the adrenalin level and can be addictive. We can look great if we solve crises that are in the public eye. But following a leader who is perpetually firefighting and problem solving is exhausting. Firefighting tends to destroy the stability which many people need to feel safe and to operate effectively. And continually dealing with crises leads to stress, burn out and death!

Shrink the urgent and important activities by spending longer on the important and influential ones.

Urgent and Important but <u>not my</u> Important/Urgent: Other people's demands on us can soak up a lot of time and distract us from doing the activities we have identified as important and influential. We often hear *"Can you just … ?"* *"Do this for me by Friday"*, *"The ExCo needs this information by end of play"* and so on. Responding immediately can be satisfying. It may distract us from something less interesting and offer validation when we receive thanks. And responding to other people may be an important part of our job. However, we will stay calmer and be more effective if we can control when we do these tasks and how many of them we accept.

These six D words will help you manage other people's important and urgent and stay sane yourself!

1. *Delay* your knee-jerk reaction. Breathe. Put yourself in a calm state of mind where you can decide how to respond. This might include saying, *"I'm in the middle of XXX, please could you come back at YYY and we can discuss how to deal with this"*.

2. *Delegate.* Give what you can back to the person who offered you the task. This will empower them and build long-term sustainability. Teaching others

how to do things they ask you to do falls into the *Important and Influential* bracket. It may take longer initially than doing the task yourself, yet, when they learn how to do it themselves, they are empowered and no longer rely on you. You no longer have to do the task for them. You use some time now to gain much more time in the future.

3. ***Disaggregate.*** Listen to what the request is (at a time that works for you) and break it down into more manageable chunks that can be spread over a longer period of time and/or distributed to a range of different people.

4. ***Diminish.*** Decide how much of the task is really essential. Sometimes a request might be for massively detailed data, when a small amount of high-quality data would be more effective.

5. ***Ditch.*** We don't have to do everything we are asked to do! Someone once said to us, *"When they ask for it the third time, I know they really want it"*. He manged to avoid duplication of tasks and to keep focused on key priorities by waiting to see if the request came back again. And sometimes it's an internal pressure we put on ourselves, maybe about the quality we expect. Good enough is often just what it says on the tin – good enough.

6. ***Disappear.*** When we go on holiday, other people get by. They pick up the project and take responsibility (growing their own ownership and skills) – or maybe some things just don't get done (and prove not to be quite so urgent or important after all). Leave the office at the end of the day in good time. Giving yourself a deadline and doing only what can be done before the deadline has a great impact on your ability to prioritise. It also allows you to jump into the fourth segment of our Disc.

Rest, Restore and Review: These activities fuel the engine and oil the mind. They are essential. We need to put the mind out of gear regularly in order to think clearly at other times.

It's not a coincidence that we often have creative ideas when walking the dog, working out, laughing with a friend. Nor should it be a surprise that sometimes we wake up in the morning with the answer to last night's problem. The mind works well when allowed to rest and play.

Sleep on it! The purposes of sleep are still not fully understood: but we know we can't do without it. If we don't have enough sleep our decisions making functions and higher thinking skills are adversely affected. A theory still under research in 2019 is that sleep allows the brain to cleanse itself, physically removing toxins and so maintaining full and clear functioning. Whatever the detailed explanations turn out to be, it's a false economy to short change ourselves of sleep.

Other types of physical activity and relaxation also restore us. Our brain functions are sharper if our other muscles are fitter. And we need the range from activity to deep relaxation. All muscles, the brain included, become stressed and less effective if overworked. So, ensure you allow yourself periods of real relaxation. Consider what gives you full relaxation. It is not the same for all of us. Relaxed states can be created by activities such as yoga, meditation and mindfulness, or by other pastimes which just absorb us so much that we become less aware both of our worries and of our bodily stresses: for instance listening to music which delights us, reading an absorbing book, looking at something beautiful.

What helps you flop and absorbs you in the moment so that mind and body unwind? Remember some triggers for this refreshing state and ensure you apply them regularly.

There's an element of detox in all of this. To function at our best, we need not just to detox from harmful substances (it's a very short-term fix to use excess alcohol to relax or caffeine to stay alert) but also to detox from digital dependency, distraction and despair. Ensure that you have regular periods when you are not available by any device. We can't unwind and become absorbed by a country walk if we are alert for emails pinging in. We can't be fully present with our children and to their feelings and sensitivities if we are waiting for a text. For real downtime, we need space free of all digital connection. And it appears that we especially need some time without the sort of blue light that comes from screens in the period just before we go to sleep if we are to get the full value of that sleep. Estimates of the ideal screen free time pre-bed vary from one to as much as three hours.

For real refreshment we also need longer periods of digital detox. A holiday break is diminished in value if we are always on alert and checking for messages and information. We should not require this of our employees and colleagues and we should not require it of ourselves. We are all more creative, moving energised into the *Important and Influential* space of the Do-It-Disc, when we have really had a break from digital demands, professional pressures and work woes.

Removing ourselves from our usual close-up view gives us enough distance and perspective to review effectively. We allow ourselves to look elsewhere and return to the usual context with fresh eyes, with the result that we may be amazed at what we see.

Sometimes we are forced to adopt a different perspective because of unexpected events or crises. Most of us will know someone whose family (and maybe colleagues) were telling them they were working too hard; not to over-do it; that they were not indispensable. Then they fell ill or burnt out, and they discovered the hard way that the advice was well founded.

Pacing ourselves, ensuring restorative activity and space allows us to keep perspective, to see other points of view. We widen our focus and recognise alternatives: in short, we are more resourced, more resilient and more creative. And we get time off, fun, rest, holidays and space. Why wouldn't we?

Attention – Task – Rest – Repeat!

As you think about the periods of rest and replenishment, it's worth checking again what we do which can lead to such a deep need to refresh. Pause when you are very busy or feel overwhelmed. *What are you doing? Is it your task? Is it a necessary task? Who says? What is its purpose? Who else could do it?*

These questions may be summed up as "*What is the contract?*" Often, when we give ourselves time to notice, we find that there is no need for us to do this thing. Or no need now.

Years ago, we coached a man who had just started his own business: it was in the early stages and he operated virtually from home. He was anxious to get started each morning and annoyed that he often only got to his desk after 9.30a.m. When we explored why, he explained that before starting he had to see everyone else off and tidy round the kitchen, put out the rubbish, etc. A few moment's consideration revealed that he would not have done that when he was setting off to work elsewhere. He would merely have left the house at the right time to arrive at work promptly. In this case he had a contract with the previous employer and had not made a contract with himself.

In considering where to place our limited attention, we benefit from taking time to focus on which tasks are important and why. We look at the task in the light of our role and responsibilities, our objectives and competing priorities. When we can clearly see the value of what we are doing and the value of our doing it (as opposed to someone else doing it), motivation is enhanced, and feelings of tedium and resentment reduced. As we become more senior in an organisation and have a bigger span of control, it's useful to adopt the maxim *"Only do what only you can do"*. If you are the only person who can sign off on a particular project, it's not a good plan for you to balance the petty cash first.

Back to the fact that you can't manage time. However, you *can* manage your attention and what you commit to, where you put your energy and how you support others to fulfil their roles.

Promoting your wellbeing

Self-care also comes from liking and reassuring yourself. Various mental practices have been shown to promote wellbeing. These include:

- Gratitude
- Positive thinking
- Reinforcement

As we mentioned in Chapter 2, research into happiness suggests that positive thinking and gratitude will help us to maintain a resourceful and satisfied state of mind.

Try telling yourself each night as you go to sleep about three things you are grateful for today and/or three things you did well today. Notice how when you start this practice your thoughts may rapidly drift to things you'd like to have done differently. This shows our tendency to correct ourselves, rather than praising and reinforcing the things which are working well. Think about dog training! We praise the good behaviour to get the animal to replicate it. Treat yourself better than a dog! Adopt the practice of self-praise (perhaps not in public!) and gratitude for the things which you have, and which go well.

Some years ago, we arrived to run one of a series of workshops with people who were very downbeat and finding it hard to motivate themselves and others.

We asked them to come up with things they were grateful for that morning (it was 09.30) and after a long silence and much prompting, they managed a few things like:

- *It's not raining.*
- *The traffic was not too heavy.*
- *I didn't have to park too far away.*

What do you notice? All in the negative. When we reframed these into the positive, we began a flow of much more positive thought and some praise and reinforcement of themselves and others. The day proceeded very differently from previous workshops.

Random acts of kindness

Gratitude helps us see things in perspective, lightens our mood, encourages outward-looking and connection. It seems to feed our level of happiness. Research into happiness also suggests that doing things for others improves not just their happiness but ours also. Indeed, we may receive the greater benefit, because it also appears to enhance our physical wellbeing.

Almost every religion and philosophy suggest that we should be kind to others: not from direct self-interest, so that they will immediately return the favour, but from a broader sense of shared humanity. And happiness studies show that there is an almost immediate personal benefit in self-worth and improved comfort.

This idea, that it is good for us to be good to others, links many of the concepts in this book: the emotional bank account, assertiveness balance where we are both OK, acceptance of others as other, flexing and fun.

When we notice what someone else needs, we are focusing outside ourselves, perhaps escaping our own pressures and pains for a moment, contextualising them. We are recognising another's otherness. We are putting things in proportion. We are thinking creatively. We are engaging with our surroundings.

We're shifting our point of view. We feel different as a result. And this enables us to interact differently. It's a virtuous spiral.

Kindness connects with and promotes gratitude, which heightens our sense of appreciation and luck. It fosters compassion and helps us to feel connected – meeting a fundamental human need. It has physiological benefits too, releasing neurochemicals which make us feel good: potentially the same effect as a chemical high. Regular acts of kindness may even boost the immune system, helping us to stay physically healthy.

No wonder there are numerous advocates of building a daily habit of random acts of kindness. So often does this occur in writing about desirable behaviour throughout the ages that it's almost as though it's hard-wired into us. Notice how many people may start forward when an old person drops their stick in a shop. Cultivating our awareness of others and their needs allows us to incorporate these small acts of grace into our daily course of life, often without much deviation for our usual pattern.

Here are some of the small things you might choose to do:

- Smile.
- Let another person/car in ahead of you in a queue.
- Send someone a thoughtful message.
- Lift someone's heavy bag for them.
- Share compliments you have overheard.
- Pay compliments yourself.
- Really listen to people.
- Give someone the benefit of the doubt.
- Share and give things: a flower, a magazine, a joke, a tear.

When some of these things become a habit, we relax and see ourselves and others in perspective more. We are not stuck in our own preoccupations and we are more likely to be optimistic, lighter in mind and spirit.

The roots of wellbeing and growth

As you reflect on ideas which have emerged as you've read (or dipped into) this book, it is likely that you'll have noticed some ideas or techniques which are useful to you in keeping you grounded and purposeful, safe and well, motivated and engaged, happy and fulfilled. These are the constituents of your own wellbeing. It underpins your ability to have a healthy understanding of who you are and a mature and self-aware approach to others.

As we reflected on the roots of wellbeing while gathering our thoughts, beliefs and ideas for the book, we came up with a symbolic tree, created here by Jessica Balla. Its roots are our suggestion of the elements that go to create a personal sense of wellbeing.

What nourishes your wellbeing?

Try drawing your own wellbeing tree!

- What are the roots of your tree?
- How do they get water and food, light and warmth?
- What's essential to your inner being?
- What keeps you strong, positive and effective at work?
- What gives you a solid basis for sound relationships and effective working?

The image of ourselves as rooted and nurtured, is reassuring and powerful. It is linguistically vivid: we talk about people being uprooted or wobbled, about needing to ground ourselves. Knowing what keeps us attached is vital to our sense of self and of wellbeing.

Burnishing your self-image

It can sometimes seem an alien notion that we need to be kind to ourselves. Yet building our own sense of ourselves as strong, resourceful and unique beings can help us not only to feel happier and more confident but can also help us to make the workplace a place of greater tolerance and equality for others. Feeling good improves our performance. In business, as in a plane, we must put our own oxygen mask on before we can help others.

A *Golden Glow* book can help us to a greater self-appreciation. This is a notebook in which you only write positive things about yourself and your experiences, and which you add to and reread on a regular basis. When you reread what you have written, it gives you an inner glow!

Try this

Choose a notebook which you really like the look and feel of.

Each day, write down verbatim appreciative comments which other people have made to you, with their names:

- Su said, *"You made a big impression in the meeting when you laid out your plan for the next quarter so clearly"*.
- Anh thanked me for my support, *"You gave me all that time on Monday and so I felt supported"*.
- Trinh said, *"You're a great friend"*.

Record times when you felt positive about yourself. You might like to draw or sketch as well as write! Maybe use different colours.

- *I confronted the lion in the den today. Quaking, but I did it!* ★ ★ ★
- *Went home on time at the end of the day. Told everyone that it could wait until tomorrow. Felt so strong.* 👍 👍
- *Lovely day choosing what I wanted to do. Took advantage of the sun and cut myself some slack.* 😊

Spend a bit of time at night reading your notebook. Allow yourself time to dwell on these good memories and feel the glow!

Back to emotional intelligence

In focusing on the influence our state of being has on our work, we realise that we've come full circle – back to where we started in this book and back to our central idea that the only person we can actually manage is ourselves.

Earlier we looked at how the essence of our personality and the way we decode and respond to the world amplifies as we interact with others. We illustrated this with our most simple cone diagram, in Chapter 2 – and here it is again, as a prompt for thinking about how your perception of your interactions with others has changed.

We have a staggering number of choices each day, almost each moment, and when we accept that and fully engage in being at choice, we have more impact around us, allow others also to be fully themselves and at choice and so can achieve things which overall seem like more than the sum of the parts.

Who/How Cone revisited

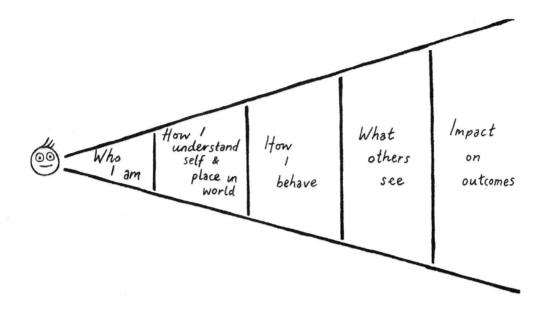

Try this

Spend a moment looking at each segment of the cone and noticing what stands out for you. There may be a space in which you would like to explore more or develop something new. There may be events which you'd like to reflect on using each section of the cone as a prompt.

- What do you now think about your place in the world?
- How does your self-perception impact on how you behave?
- What conclusions might other people draw as a result of how you behave?
- How might this be impacting on your working relationships?
- How might this in turn be affecting the outcomes you achieve individually/ together?
- What might lead to a different set of behaviours?
- What would you actually like other people to see?
- If this happened, what would the impact be?
- So, what might you choose to believe/do differently?

Intuition

So, the body tells the story, manifesting the intricate connection of body and mind. When we function at our best, we're allowing all parts of ourselves to contribute to how we work, the logical, physical, emotional. And then there is this thing which people call intuition.

What is intuition? It may seem to be something rather intangible and beyond our comprehension. We, that is, Jenny and Sarah, believe that intuition is a full integration of all our senses, possible when we are well resourced and comfortable in and with ourselves. It's a fusion of all we are capable of, of the capacities which we can lose when we are overworked, overstretched or overloaded. It permits us to access knowledge and experience in a non-rational way, totally appropriately to the context.

We know that over millennia humans have lost senses which animals retain, for instance sensing when the weather is changing. Animals sense a tsunami coming through their feet as they sense the vibration of the earth. And if we are settled in ourselves and in flow, we are able to synthesise sources of information at an astounding rate, and to have the lightening recognitions which we call intuition. We have a sudden sense of knowing and can voice a truth apparently not logically available to us before.

Here is how we understand different aspects of intuition. When we are accessing our intuition, we are able to synthesise:

Observation: We're picking up a huge range of things from the way a person moves, gestures, sits, holds themselves; their use of space and their environment; from the weather and the plants, traffic, buildings.

Relation: We're using human (and animal) sensing of the other and sympathy for feelings and experiences. We are operating at a sensory level.

Information: We're able to hold factors from the news, information about families, background, illness, education, systemic factors, cultural codes, local practices … .

The intuitive self

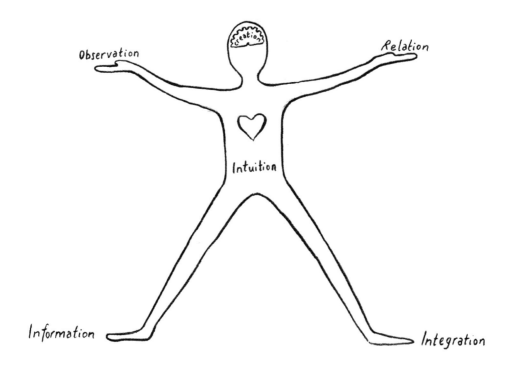

Integration: We're able to connect all this diverse data, at a subconscious level, without working it through step by step. The integrated understanding is greater than the logical sum of the parts.

Creation: Integrating stimulates the potential for an imaginative jump to a completely fresh interpretation, drawing on all our senses, interpersonal skills, emotional intelligence and logical abilities.

Intuition: When we are working with intuition, we can rapidly access the gut, that deeper sense of visceral knowledge. We have enough body and head space to do this. We draw on all aspects of ourselves as we offer insights or behave in ways which we have not consciously thought through. When we find that the result is full of impact, we develop the intuition muscle and, with experience, learn to trust what our gut is telling us.

In summary, we can access our intuition when we are in a place of wellbeing because we are able to respond with every part of ourselves, accessing information from body, mind, emotions, different senses, what we see and hear. It's an expression of our fullest possibility when we allow ourselves the level of wellbeing which makes it possible to access and share our intuition.

Which leads to ...

We have come full circle, back to the self.

Everything in our lives, including our work, begins and ends with us and is filtered through our perceptions of how things are.

And in everything we have opportunities to make choices that minimise interference and maximise our potential.

As we become more aware about ourselves, our own processing and behaviours, we become more open to accepting others, accommodating their differences and perceptions and working with them constructively towards better results!

We can learn to flex our behaviours producing new outcomes and connections. We can adopt a range of techniques and approaches to fit the person and situation. We can dance in the moment and develop skill, confidence and shared achievement.

Potential + Awareness – Interference = Amplified Results!

So, we return to this equation. What have your ideas, experiments and reflections changed for you?

Read on for reminders and more to explore …

How to work with people … and enjoy it!

✪   Develop honest self-knowledge.

✪   Shift your self-perception, attitudes and behaviours.

✪   Accept that other people are not like you: you're OK and they're OK.

✪   Believe in yourself: be who you truly are.

✪   Challenge assumptions and make new choices.

✪   Recognise, explore and reframe limiting beliefs.

✪   Balance ego states.

✪   Pay credit into the emotional bank account.

✪   Recognise your own preferences; work with other people's.

✪   Suit the leadership style to the person and circumstances.

✪   Adapt your language and behaviour to be appropriate for each person.

✪   Catch people doing good things: offer specific praise.

✪   Explore your triggers, stories and baggage.

✪   Recognise old hooks: choose new behaviours.

✪   Clarify roles; honour responsibilities; maintain healthy boundaries.

✪   Know you have a choice.

✪   Accept change: welcome learning.

✪   Manage stakeholders, focus effort.

✪   Believe in win–win: work for it.

✪   Make clear decisions: keep hope.

✪   Prioritise the important and influential.

✪   Respect, refresh and restore mind and body.

✪   Honour your own unique value.

Chapter 8

References and further reading

References and further reading

Many models in this book are original to Jenny Bird and Sarah Gornall. The illustrations were created by Jess Balla, often based on sketches by Sarah Gornall, though some are re-drawings of illustrations created by Josie Vallely in *The Art of Coaching: A Handbook of Tips and Tools,* Jenny and Sarah's earlier co-authored book.

This chapter contains:
- Some background information
- References where we have mentioned other published works
- Options for reading further if you would like to follow up on ideas, theory or research

It is an indication of where you might like to start your own research, rather than an exhaustive reading list.

Bird, J. and Gornall, S. (2016). *The Art of Coaching: A Handbook of Tips and Tools.* Abingdon: Routledge.

Chapter 1

The technological dream

Maynard Keynes suggested in 1930 that, as a result of automation, people a century on, so in 2030, would spend only 15 hours a week working.

More recently, prominent thinkers at the World Economic Forum have described the concept of the Fourth Industrial Revolution, a time when cyber-physical systems offer new possibilities for integrating technology in our ways of working, our machines and even our bodies. Nicholas Davies, Head of Society of and Innovation for the World Economic Forum, posed the question of whether these new technologies are *"tools that we can identify, grasp and consciously use … or … enablers that influence our perception of the world, change our behaviour and affect what it means to be human?"* (2016).

The contention in this book is that despite technology, we remain human and have the ability within ourselves to choose how to be more fully so, aware and interacting with others in a mutually enriching way.

Davis, N. (2016). What is the Fourth Industrial Revolution? Retrieved from www.weforum.org/agenda/2016/01/what-is-the-fourth-industrial-revolution

Keynes, M. (1930). Economic Possibilities for our Grandchildren. Republished (1963). In *Essays in Persuasion.* New York: W.W. Norton & Co.

Schwab, K. (2016). *The Fourth Industrial Revolution.* Geneva: World Economic Forum.

Schwab, K. (2017). *The Fourth Industrial Revolution.* New York: Crown Business.

Disaffection at work

Anecdotally, there are many differing reports of the degree of dissatisfaction/satisfaction with work. These are backed up by a range of surveys conducted by different organisations. The American company Gallup runs a worldwide annual survey on employee engagement, which it defines as a measure of involvement, enthusiasm and commitment to work. This survey, the State of the Global Workplace, reported in 2017 that 85% of employees were not engaged or were actively disengaged at work. With 67% not engaged and 18% actively disengaged, only 15% were engaged with work.

This reported percentage was very similar in each of the preceding five years. There are huge implications for organisational performance, of course, but more importantly, we consider, implications for human misery.

Potential – Interference = Results

Myles Downey suggests, in his seminal book *Effective Coaching*, that coaching develops two things, potential and performance, and that performance is enhanced when interference is reduced. This is also the premise at the heart of Tim Gallwey's writing about the Inner Game: the internal work on the mind and attitudes which underpins a shift in behaviour and performance.

Our use of the word "results" suggests for us a wider scope. At work *"performance management"* has often been used as a term for measuring the effectiveness of employees' work. A performance management system may include challenging objectives and pay related bonuses. The effort to meet unrealistic annual objectives accompanied by fear of consequences if they are not met, can lead to stress in the workplace. This book focuses instead on a wider range of results, intrapersonal and interpersonal.

Downey, M. (1999). *Effective Coaching*. London: Texere.

Gallwey, T. (1975). *The Inner Game of Tennis*. London: Pan Macmillan.

Gallwey, T. (2000). *The Inner Game of Work*. New York: Random House.

Six people in a conversation

Chrisafis, A and Berger, J. (2017). Guterres brings all-round élan to the UN. Manchester. *Guardian Weekly* (06.01.2017).

Copyright Guardian News & Media Ltd. 2018

Chapter 2

Who/How Cone

The *Who/How Cone* is a development of the *Emotional Intelligence Cone* diagram created by Jenny Bird and Sarah Gornall for *The Art of Coaching: A Handbook of Tips and Tools*. We hope that as a diagrammatic tool it enables us to understand more clearly the relationship between how we see ourselves, how others see us, how we choose to behave and what we achieve, both for ourselves and with those around us.

The concept of emotional intelligence is helpful when we seek to understand and impact on relational behaviour. It has been described in the work of Daniel Goleman, although it was Howard Gardner who put forward the theory that there are multiple forms or presentations of intelligence in the 1980s.
These include the interpersonal (intelligence about what's going on between people) and the intrapersonal (intelligence about what's going on inside ourselves).

The idea of multiple forms of intelligence has been highly debated since and has been impacted by new findings in the world of neuroscience.

Bird, J. and Gornall, S. (2016). *The Art of Coaching: A Handbook of Tips and Tools*. Abingdon: Routledge.

Gardner, H. (1983). *Frames of Mind: The Theory of Multiple Intelligences*. London: Fontana.

Goleman, D. (1995). *Emotional Intelligence*. New York: Bantam Books.

Goleman, D. (2002). *Primal Leadership: Realizing the Power of Emotional Intelligence*. Boston: Harvard Business School Press.

Goleman D. (2006). *Social Intelligence*. New York: Hutchinson.

There are many fascinating books on neuroscience, the scientific study of the nervous system, which illuminate how the brain influences our behaviour, including:

Brann, A. (2013). *Make Your Brain Work*. London: Kogan Page.

Brown P. and Brown V. (2012). *Neuropsychology for Coaches*. Maidenhead: OUP.

Rock, D. (2009). *Your Brain at Work*. New York: Harper Collins.

Self-fulfilling prophecy

Though references to our responses having a reinforcing effect on situations appear from very early writings, the term *"Self-Fulfilling Prophesy"* is attributed to American sociologist Robert Merton.

Merton, Robert K. (1948). The Self-Fulfilling Prophecy. *Antioch Review, 8* (2).

Positive and negative cycles of thought

Sigmund Freud laid the foundations for the way that many people today think about the interactions of mind, emotions, personality and motivations (psychodynamics). How we experience stimuli and interpret them is closely entangled with how we feel, react and are seen by others to behave.

The field of cognitive psychology helps us to explore how our minds create patterns of thinking and internal dialogue in response to external stimuli. The language we use, as we talk to ourselves, shapes our map of reality. When we pick these patterns apart, we can often uncover chains of assumptions and unchallenged beliefs. Then we have new awareness, which can be the springboard for creating a fresh way of thinking and reacting, which may be more desirable to us or more effective in our relationships at work or at home. Awareness gives us choice.

A framework for changing internal dialogue might follow the following steps:

A. Clarify the event that activated the chain of thoughts and feelings.
B. Identify beliefs and assumptions underlying these thoughts.
C. Identify consequences of the thoughts, in terms of feelings and behaviour.
D. Dispute the ineffective self-limiting and negative beliefs.
E. Build an effective chain of thoughts, feelings and actions.

There is an example of using a cognitive behavioural framework to change a pattern of thought using analytical questioning in Sarah Gornall and Mannie Burns' book on coaching in schools.

Beck, A. (1976). *Cognitive Therapy and the Emotional Disorders*. New York: Grove Press.

Briers, S. (2009). *Brilliant Cognitive Behavioural Therapy*. Harlow: Pearson

Butler-Bowdon, T. (2007). *50 Psychology Classics*. London: Nicholas Brearley.

Ellis, A. and Harper, R. (1975). *A New Guide to Rational Living*. Englewood Cliffs, New Jersey: Prentice-Hall.

Freud, A. (1948). *The Ego and the Mechanisms of Defence*. London: The Hogarth Press.

Gornall, S. and Burn, M. (2013). *Coaching and Learning in Schools: A Practical Guide*. London: Sage.

Positive thinking

Many writers and researchers in the field of Positive Psychology refer to the effect of positive thinking on state of mind. Positive Psychology focuses on optional functioning, rather than dysfunction, and research in this area identifies aspects of our thinking, attributes and interactions which can lead to people and organisations flourishing.

While Positive Psychology is a new discipline, the idea that we can choose thoughts which impact on our experience of the world, was also powerfully described by Viktor Frankl, an Austrian psychiatrist and Holocaust survivor. His book, *Man's Search for Meaning,* originally published in 1946, has been republished more recently and his thinking has gained wider currency.

Frankl is widely quoted as saying:

- *When we are no longer able to change a situation, we are challenged to change ourselves.*
- *Between stimulus and response there is a space. In that space is our power to choose our response. In our response lies our growth and our freedom.*

Emile Coué proposed the use of autosuggestion to embed habits of positive thinking. He likens the imagination to a torrent, which, if left to its own devices, might destroy everything in its path. If directed and focused, its power can be harnessed, providing drive, heat and electricity. The English phrase *"Every day in every way I am getting better and better"* is a popular translation of Coué's original French *"Tous les jours à tous points de vue je vais de mieux en mieux"*.

Boniwell, I. (2006). *Positive Psychology in a Nutshell*. London: PWBC.

Coué, E. (1921). *Self Mastery through Conscious Autosuggestion*. (Van Orden, A.S., Trans.). New York: Malkan Publishing (http:/books.google.com).

Frankl, V. (2006). *Man's Search for Meaning*. Boston: Beacon Press.

Seligman, M.E.P. (2006). *Learned Optimism: How to Change Your Mind and Your Life*. New York: Vintage Books.

Integrity in leadership

We mention that what people most want from their leaders is honesty. This assertion is based on the work of Jim Kouzes and Barry Posner who have researched leadership qualities for over 30 years.

Sharing your vulnerability is one way of becoming real to your followers and demonstrating the authenticity that they value.

Kouzes, J and Posner, B. (2008). *The Leadership Challenge* (4th ed.). San Francisco, California: Jossey–Bass.

Brown, B. (2012). *Daring Greatly: How the Courage to be Vulnerable Transforms the Way We Live, Love, Parent and Lead*. New York: Gotham Books.

Chapter 3

Tells

Collett, P. (2004). *The Book of Tells*. London: Bantam.

Mehrabian, A. (1971). *Silent Messages*. Belmont, California: Wadsworth.

Virtuous spirals

Virtuous spirals, as opposed to vicious circles, take us on a positive upward trajectory of thought, as described in our previous book, *The Art of Coaching: A Handbook of Tips and Tools*. Both are processes where once we are caught up, there is an impetus leading us in the same direction, maybe without our noticing initially what is happening. Sketching out these patterns and asking where we see ourselves, what the energy is, what we would like to be different and how we could start to turn the process around, will help us to shift from one pattern to the other.

Johari Window

This representation of the Johari Window has been redrawn from Josie Vallely's illustration in *The Art of Coaching: A Handbook of Tips and Tools*, which in turn uses the same names for the various segments of the model as in Bruce Peltier's work *The Psychology of Executive Coaching*.

Bird, J. and Gornall, S. (2016). *The Art of Coaching: A Handbook of Tips and Tools*. Abingdon: Routledge.

Hanson, P. (1973). The Johari Window: A Model for Soliciting and Giving Feedback. In Jones J and Pfeiffer P. W. (Eds.), (1973). *The 1973 Annual Handbook for Facilitators*. San Diego, California: Pfeiffer & Company.

Luft, J. (1970). *Group Processes: An Introduction to Group Dynamics*. (2nd ed.). Palo Alto, California: National Press Books.

Peltier, B. (2001). *The Psychology of Executive Coaching*. Abingdon: Routledge.

Transactional analysis

Transactional Analysis, or TA, lies within the humanist tradition of psychology. As mentioned in the text, it originates in the work of Eric Berne, and gives us frameworks for understanding what's going on inside our own minds and between us and other people (the intrapersonal and interpersonal, mentioned earlier in the Chapter 2 reference for the Emotional Intelligence Cone). The underlying philosophy is that people are OK – that is, they have worth and integrity as human beings. They have the capacity to think, make decisions about their destiny and change those decisions. TA gives us the concepts of scripts, life positions, ego states and the Drama and Winners' Triangles.

Berne, E. (1964). *Games People Play – The Psychology of Human Relationships*. London: Penguin.

Cochrane, H. and Newton, T. (2018). *Supervision and Coaching*. Abingdon: Routledge.

Harris, T. (1969). *I'm OK, You're OK: A Practical Guide to Transactional Analysis*. New York: Harper and Row.

Hay, J. (1993). *Working it Out at Work*. Watford: Sherwood Publishing.

Napper, R. and Newton, T. (2000). *TACTICS*. Ipswich: TA Resources.

Stewart, I. and Joines, V. (1987). *T.A. Today*. Nottingham: Lifespan Publishing.

Scarcity and abundant thinking

Dweck, C. (2012). *Mindset: How You Can Fulfil Your Potential*. New York: Random House.

Hill, N. (1937). *Think and Grow Rich!* New York: Barnes & Noble.

Chapter 4

Different preferences

The grandfather of work on personality types was Carl Jung, the eminent Swiss psychologist and psychoanalyst. His seminal book *Psychological Types* was originally published in 1921, and has been republished more recently. Jung likens the meeting of two personalities to the contact between two chemical substances. Each different, they have the potential to transform each other.

As different people react differently to each other, we find that at work, there is an impact on the wider team as well. We need these different personalities and diversity to make a rounded team. The varying perspectives and approaches contribute to a more multilayered view and more effective solutions, increasing the chances of success.

But only of course, if we take into account other people's preferences for learning and for operating.

Belbin, R.M. (1981). *Management Teams: Why they Succeed or Fail.* Oxford: Butterworth-Heinemann.

Honey, P. and Mumford, A. (1982). *Manual of Learning Styles.* London: Peter Honey.

Jung, C.G. (1971). *Psychological Types.* Oxford: Harcourt, Brace.

DISC – An example of a diagnostic tool for working with preferences

There are a number of providers who run workshops in DISC, or who provide materials for DISC profiling. An internet search will give you choice!

Marston, W. (1928). *Emotions of Normal People.* Abingdon: Routledge, Trench, Trubner & Co. Ltd.

MBTI® – An example of a diagnostic tool for working with preferences

Myers-Briggs Type Indicator® and MBTI® are registered UK and US Trademarks of Consulting Psychologists Press Inc (CPP). Training in the UK is provided by OPP, part of CPP – the Myers-Briggs® Company and one of Europe's largest business psychology providers. Contact OPP if you are interested in training as an MBTI® practitioner.

Briggs Myers, I. with Myers, P. (1995). *Gifts Differing: Understanding Personality Types.* Palo Alto, California: Davies-Black.

Briggs Myers, I. (revised by Kirby, L.K. and Myers, K.D.) (2000). *Introduction to Type®.* Oxford: OPP.

Kiersey, D. (1998). *Please Understand Me.* Delmar: Prometheus Nemesis Book Company.

Rogers, J. (1997). *Sixteen Personality Types at Work in Organisations.* London: Management Futures.

Linguistic adjustments; mismatched communication

The linguistic habits that we develop are indicators of how we organise our beliefs and interpret the world. They determine how we put out our communication. Other people have different linguistic habits and a different interpretation of the world. They receive our communication through the medium of their own linguistic and belief filters, which may lead them to discard or disregard some of the message we intended to send.

The study of communication, which emerged in the 20th century, identified this universal problem of a shift in the exact nature of a message on the journey between sender and receiver. The field has moved from a technological focus on medium and transmission to taking into account types of influence and interference which are human and psychological.

The way we are programmed by our habits, and our potential to change our programming, are explored in the literature of Neuro-Linguistic Programming, more widely known as NLP. This brings together ideas from a number of disciplines, including psychotherapy, linguistics and hypnotherapy and offers practical exercises for changing the way we see the world, talk about our involvement within it and act. NLP originates from the work of Richard Bandler and John Grinder, working in the USA in the 1970s.

Adler, H. (1994). *NLP – The New Art and Science of Getting What You Want.* London: Piatkus.

Bandler, R. and Grinder, J. (1975, 1976). *The Structure of Magic: A book about Language and Therapy (vols. 1 & 2).* Palo Alto, California: Science and Behavior Books.

Bateson, G. (1972). *Steps to an Ecology of Mind.* Chicago, Illinois: University of Chicago Press.

Dilts, R. (1990). *Changing Belief Systems with NLP.* Capitol, California: Meta Publications.

Fiske, J. (1990). *An Introduction to Communication Studies.* London: Routledge.

Ready, R. and Burton, K. (2004). *Neuro-Linguistic Programming for Dummies.* Chichester: John Wiley.

Weaver, W. and Shannon, C.E. (1963). *The Mathematical Theory of Communication.* Champion, Illinois: University of Illinois Press.

Praise as a motivator

Using praise as a motivator, in small and immediate chunks, is one of the tenets of Levy, the effective manager in *The One Minute Manager*. He puts forward the following motto: *"Help People Reach Their Full Potential – Catch Them Doing Something Right"*.

Blanchard, K. and Johnson, S. (1983). *The One Minute Manager*. Glasgow: Fontana/Collins.

Dog training

As we are no experts on dog training ourselves, nor indeed even dog-owners, we have sourced this information from the website of the Dogs Trust Ltd. (GB) www.dogstrust.org.uk.

Leadership style

Hersey, P. and Blanchard, K. (1982). *Situational Leadership: A Summary*. San Diego, California: University Associates.

Drama, Winners' and Social Roles Triangles

The Drama, Winners' and Social Roles Triangles all offer models for the way we interact with other people. The thinking that has led to them draws on analysis of folk tales and myths through the ages and across different cultures. Myths, both ancient and modern, have a potent impact on our view of our role in life and influence how we interpret what happens to us and what we "ought" to do.

While the Drama and Winners' Triangles are more widely known, Agnès Le Guernic suggests that there must be a normal triangle: –a Social Roles Triangle. The beneficial roles she describes are those of the Guide, or person who stimulates action in others (Mandateur); Helper (Donneur); and Hero or Beneficiary, who receives help and guidance from others (Bénéficiaire). In this concept, we are all beneficiaries and heroes of our own stories. We all need to learn to accept help from others and to grow into giving help ourselves.

The habits we adopt, or roles we grow into, are also formed by how we learn to behave in order to thrive at a young age. We set off on our life's journey with good intent, informed by the interactions we observe around us between the people who are significant to us. When these ways of behaviour are rewarded by others, that is, when we benefit in some way from using them, they become reinforced and we repeat them without conscious choice. Familial patterns can be reinforced across the centuries.

Sometimes the patterns we develop do not continue to serve us or those around us well. We may not notice that this is the case. Information about our behaviour may be in the blind area of the Johari window and we may need someone to help us see and support us if we choose to change.

Choy, A. (1990). The Winners' Triangle. *Transactional Analysis Journal, 20* (1).

Karpman, K. (1968). Fairy Tales and Script Drama Analysis. *Transactional Analysis Journal, 7* (26).

Le Guernic, A. (2004). Fairy Tales and Psychological Life Plans. *Transactional Analysis Journal, 34* (3).

Le Guernic, A. (2016). Snow White: The Triumph of Beauty. In Barrow G.and Newton. T. (2016). *Educational Transactional Analysis: An International Guide to Theory and Practice*. Abingdon: Routledge.

Chapter 5

Stories we tell ourselves

The 100% versus 60 % statistic in relation to how women and men represent themselves, comes from an internal report at Hewlett Packard quoted in an article by Georges DesVaux et al. and colleagues in the McKinsey Quarterly in 2008 and requoted by Sheryl Sandberg in *Lean In*. It was followed up in personal research with over 1,000 people by Tara Mohr, who discovered that the top reasons for not applying for a job for both men and women were *"I didn't think they would hire me since I didn't meet the qualifications"* and *"I didn't want to waste my time and energy"*.

Desvaux, G., Devillard–Hoellinger, S., and Meaney, M.C. (2008). A Business Case for Women. In *The McKinsey Quarterly*. Seattle, Washington. Retrieved from www.mckinsey.com

Mohr, T. (2014). *Playing Big: Practical Wisdom for Women Who Want to Speak Up, Create and Lead*. New York: Gotham Books.

Mohr, T. (2014). Why Women Don't Apply for Jobs Unless They're 100% Qualified. *Harvard Business Review blog*.

Sandberg, S. (2015). *Lean In*. London: WH Allen.

Seven plus or minus two

"Seven plus or minus two" was proposed as the number of randomly ordered, meaningful items or chunks of information by George Miller of Harvard University in 1956.

More recent research by Nelson Cowan, of Missouri University, has shown that the real limit of our working memory storage capacity may be three to five meaningful items.

Cowan, N. (2010). The Magical Mystery Four: How is Working Memory Capacity Limited, and Why? *Current Directions in Psychological Science, 19* (1): 51–57.

Miller, G. (1956). The Magical Number Seven, Plus or Minus Two: Some Limits on our Capacity for Processing Information. *Psychological Review*, 63: 81–97.

Assertiveness

When we are assertive, we are self-assured and confident, though not aggressive. We affirm our rights without threatening the rights of other people. One popular early text, Robert Alberti's and Michael Emmons' *Your Perfect Right*, a triumph of self-publishing in 1970, has been recently updated and republished. Anne Dickson's work is also very relevant.

Alberti, R.E. and Emmons M.L. (2017). *Your Perfect Right* (10th ed.). Oakland, California: Impact Publishing.

Dickson, A. (1982). *A Woman in Your Own Right* (30th anniversary edition (2012)). London: Quartet Books.

Being OK

Thomas A. Harris wrote a book called *I'm OK – You're OK* though this phrase is not uniquely his and is widely used in the field of Transactional Analysis – of which more above, in the references for Chapter 3.

Harris, T. (1969). *I'm OK, You're OK: A Practical Guide to Transactional Analysis*. New York: Harper & Row.

Reactions to imagined power

Schlitz, D. (1976). "The Gambler".

This song was written in 1976 and more than one version was recorded on vinyl before it became famous in a version sung by Kenny Rogers in 1978 for the American label, United Artists, (produced by Larry Butler).

NLP, Neuro-Linguistic Programming, where *Neuro* relates to the nervous system and our senses; *Linguistic* relates to language, communication and linguistic interpretation of the world; *Programming* relates to our habits. NLP is referenced in the section of this chapter that relates to Chapter 4.

Win-win technique

Cornelius, H. and Faire, S. (1989). *Everyone Can Win*. East Roseville, New South Wales: Simon & Schuster.

Leimdorfer, T. (1992). *Once Upon a Conflict: Fairy Tale Manual of Conflict Resolution for All Ages*. London: Quaker Peace and Service.

Staying balanced in the face of harassment

Jeffers, S. (1991). *Feel the Fear and Do It Anyway*. Arrow Books: London.

Chapter 6

The change process

The diagram representing the stages of the change process is based on an illustration by Josie Vallely, which appeared first in *The Art of Coaching: A Handbook of Tips and Tools* by Jenny Bird and Sarah Gornall. This was based in turn on a sketch by Sarah Gornall, as an interpretation of work by Elizabeth Kübler-Ross.

Kübler-Ross, E. (1989). *On Death and Dying*. London: Routledge.

Phillips, J.R. (1983). Enhancing the Effectiveness of Organizational Change Management. *Human Resource Management, 22* (1/2): 183–199.

Rogers, E.M. (1962). *Diffusion of Innovations*. Glencoe, Illinois: Free Press.

Conscious/unconscious steps of competence

The term *"Conscious Competence"* has been used widely to describe a stage in the development of learning. It can be traced back to articles by Martin Broadwell (1969) and W. Lewis Robinson (1974) and the work of Gordon Training International in the 1970s.

Broadwell, M.M. (1969). Teaching for Learning. *Gospel Guardian*, *20* (41): 1–3.

Robinson, W.L. (1974). Conscious Competency – The Mark of a Competent Instructor. *The Personnel Journal*, 538–539.

VUCA

V = Volatile
U = Uncertain
C = Complex
A = Ambiguous

The term VUCA derives from the leadership theories of Warren Bennis and Burt Nanus. It appears that the acronym was first used in 1987. It was applied by the USA military to the more complex conditions after the Cold War and came into more general business use in the early 2000s to describe how people experience the operating conditions of organisations.

Bennis, W. and Nanus, B. (1985). *Leaders: Strategies for Taking Charge*. New York: Harper & Row.

Reactions to threat

Eisenberger, N.I. and Lieberman, M.D. (2004). Why it Hurts to be Left Out: The Cognitive Overlap Between Physical and Social Pain. *Trends in Cognitive Sciences*, 8.

Rock, D. (2008). SCARF: A Brain-Based Model for Collaborating with and Influencing Others. *NeuroLeadership Journal*, 1.

Making and communicating decisions

"Any decision is better than no decision" is a version of a quote from Brian Tracy in his entertaining book on stopping procrastinating and getting more done in less time.

Tracy, B. (2001). *Eat That Frog!* San Francisco, California: Berrett-Koehler Publishers Inc.

Cartesian questions

The Cartesian Questions are named after the French philosopher Renée Descartes (1596–1650), who has been called the "father of modern philosophy". Rather than believing in generally accepted views, he applied his mind to working out evidence by a process of rational reasoning. The ability to think was for him a vital human attribute, summarised as *Cogito, ergo sum* (*I think, therefore I am*).

Mapping influence with objects/tactile imagoes

Cochrane, H. and Newton, T. (2011). *Supervision for Coaches.* Ipswich: Supervision for Coaches Publishing.

Whittington, J. (2012). *Systemic Coaching and Constellations: An Introduction to the Principles, Practices and Application.* London: Kogan Page

Chapter 7

Happiness

The study of happiness relates to Positive Thinking, referenced in Chapter 2.

Grenville Cleave, B., Boniwell, I., and Tessina, T.B. (2008). *The Happiness Equation.* Avon, Massachusetts: Adams Media.

Layard, R. (2004). *Happiness: Lessons from a New Science.* London: Penguin.

The body tells the story

Van der Kolk, B. (2015). *The Body Keeps the Score.* London: Penguin.

Do-It-Disc

The first model of the Do-It-Disc is described in the *Art of Coaching: A Handbook of Tips and Tools* (Bird and Gornall, 138–39). The concept of dividing problems into urgent and important seems to have gained currency after a speech given by President Eisenhower at an Assembly of the World Council of Churches in 1954, in which he quoted a college Principal as saying *"I have two kinds of problems, the urgent and the important. The urgent are not important, and the important are never urgent"*.

This has been requoted in various forms, including in Stephen Covey's time management matrix.

Bird, J. and Gornall, S. (2016). *The Art of Coaching: A Handbook of Tips and Tools.* Abingdon: Routledge.

Covey, S.R. (1989). *The 7 Habits of Highly Effective People.* London: Simon & Schuster.

Tracy, B. (2001). *Eat That Frog!* San Francisco, California: Berrett-Koehler Publishers Inc.

Quote Investigator. Retrieved from http://quoteinvestigator.com/2014/05/09/urgent/.

Sleep

Research by Xie and colleagues published in 2013 suggested that the space between brain cells may increase during sleep, allowing fluid to flow through the brain and flush out toxic molecules. This research on mice was widely reported both on the internet and by the media at the time, and some people have extrapolated implications for human neurological health.

Studies of the reasons behind decline in the average quality and length of sleep reported in many countries have shown that using electronic devices in the period immediately before sleep has a negative impact. This may be due to the short-wavelength enriched light, called *"blue light"* by some people, and extends to the use of e-readers. See recent research by Anne-Marie Chang, of Harvard University.

Chang, A., Aeschbach, D., Duffy, J.F., and Czeisler, C.A. (2015). Evening Use of Light-Emitting eReaders Negatively Affects Sleep, Circadian Timing, and Next-Morning Alertness. *PNAS*, *112* (4) 1232–1237; published ahead of print December 22, 2014. Retrieved from https://doi.org/10.1073/pnas.1418490112.

Xie, L., Kang, H., Xu Q., Chen, M.J., Liao, Y., Thiyagarajan M., O'Donnell, J., Christensen, D.J., Nicholson, C., Iliff, J.J., Takano, T., Deane, R. and Nedergaard, M. (2013). Sleep Initiated Fluid Flux Drives Metabolite Clearance from the Adult Brain. *Science*, *342* (6156): 373–377.

Random acts of kindness

Hamilton, D.R. (2010). *Why Kindness is Good for You*. London: Hay House.

Index